Alive to THRIVE

ALSO PUBLISHED BY DAWN PUBLISHING

The Trilogy of Life Itself by Dawn Bates:
Friday Bridge – Becoming a Muslim, Becoming Everyone's Business (2nd Edition, 2017)
Walaahi – A First-hand Account of Living Through the Egyptian Uprising and Why I Walked Away From Islaam (2017)
Crossing The Line – A Journey of Purpose and Self-Belief (2017)

The Sacral Series by Dawn Bates:
Moana – One Woman's Journey Back to Self (2020)
Leila – A Life Renewed One Canvas at a Time (2020)
Pandora – Melting the Ice One Dive at a Time (2021)
Alpha – Saving Humanity One Vagina at a Time (2021)

The Democ-Chu Series by Nath Brye:
Slave Boy (2020)
BloodChild (2021)

Becoming Annie – The Biography of a Curious Woman by Dawn Bates (2020)
Becoming the Champion – V1 Awareness by Korey Carpenter (2020)
Unlocked by Carmelle Crinnion (2020)
Break Down to Wake Up by Jocelyn Bellows (2020)
Standing in Strength: Inspirational Stories of Power Unleashed (2021)
The Recipe: A US Marine's Mindset to Success by Jake Cosme (2021)
The Potent Power of Menopause: A Culturally Diverse Perspective of Feminine Transformation by Dawn Bates and Clarissa Kristjansson (2022)

LIFE AFTER ATTEMPTING SUICIDE

Our Stories

Alive to THRIVE

CURATED BY
DEBBIE DEBONAIRE

© 2022 Dawn Bates & Debbie Debonaire

Published by Dawn Publishing
www.dawnbates.com

The moral right of the authors has been asserted.

For quantity sales or media enquiries, please contact the publisher at the website address above.

Cataloguing-in-Publication entry is available from the British Library.

ISBN: 978-1-913973-12-4 (paperback)
        978-1-913973-13-1 (hardback)
        978-1-913973-34-6 (ebook)

Book cover design: Alexander Von Ness
Interior Layout: Olivier Darbonville

All rights reserved. No part of this book may be reproduced, stored in a retrieval system, communicated or transmitted in any form or by means without written permission. All inquiries should be made to the publisher at the above address.

Disclaimer: The material in this publication is of the nature of general comment only and does not represent professional advice. It is not intended to provide specific guidance for particular circumstances and should not be relied on as the basis for any decision to take action or not to take action on any matters which it covers.

To discover more about Dawn Bates, the founder of Dawn Publishing, and the latest book releases, competitions and offers make sure you sign up for her regular weekly- ish emails using https://dawnbates.com/dive-in

Are you a writer? Do you want to get published? Then make sure you visit the home of Dawn Publishing at https://dawnbates.com/writers and see how Dawn can help you on your journey to becoming published!

Dedicated to

I dedicate this book firstly to my son Adam without whom this would never have been possible.

Secondly to all of those who have or who are dealing with the effects of negative mental health issues and/or suicide, whether personally or through a family member, friend or work colleague.

My heartfelt love goes out to you all.

Debbie

CONTENTS

Gratitude   ix
Disclaimer   x
Today Was the Day My Light Ran Out.   xi
Foreword   1

Debbie Debonaire 5
THE STORM BEFORE THE CALM
Reflections.. 25-27

Dawn Bates 29
MORE THAN MY NAME
Reflections.. 49-51

Cheryl Blunt 53
OUT OF IT
Reflections..68-69

Kim Levings 71
RETHINK YOU - TO LIVE THE LIFE YOU ARE CREATED TO LIVE
Reflections.. 93-95

Neringa Brand 97
GRIEF AS THE SAVING GRACE
Reflections.. 118-119

Erica Lopez **121**
OVERCOMING THE LOWEST MOMENT IN MY LIFE
Reflections.. 143-145

Tamar Medford **147**
PAIN TO PURPOSE
Reflections.. 168-169

Sandra Chaney **171**
WHEN I WAKE UP, I CHOOSE ME
Reflections.. 182-183

Melba Stetz **185**
KILLING ME SOFTLY TO BEAM ME UP, SCOTTY!
Reflections.. 199-201

Vanessa Johnson **203**
NO ONE HEARD MY CRY EXCEPT SUICIDE
Reflections.. 211-213

About the Publisher   214

GRATITUDE

I would like to give thanks to all of those who have made this book possible.

To my son, who is the pivotal reason that I changed my life around.

Gratitude goes to my three close friends, Maria, Jackie and Anna who were there for me in my darkest of times.

To Jenni who came into my life and guided me on a further transformation.

A huge thank you to my fellow authors here within, who have opened themselves to share vulnerability and their stories.

Grateful to my author coach and publisher Dawn Bates who saw something in me and whose encouragement enabled me to bring my dream to fruition.

Also, thanks to my clients past and present, and all those who have supported me along the way.

Lastly, I would like to give gratitude to myself for allowing myself to share my story as you will see inside this book, and for giving myself permission to be vulnerable.

DISCLAIMER

This disclaimer is for everyone who reads this book.

The chapters in this book are the experiences and life stories of each of the authors therein, who came together to share very deep and personal challenges in the hope that by talking about suicide from various cultural and social viewpoints, the stigma associated with suicide, and the lifestyles shared, can be lessened.

The book is written as an inspirational guide and support for those who may have been affected by suicide, directly and indirectly, and how each of the authors transformed their own individual lives.

By sharing the stories, tips and techniques each of the authors used for their own healing journey, the hope is this book will prevent more lives being ended.

Our intention is for this book to be a supportive tool both for individuals, their families, charities and organisations who work in suicide prevention, as well as the education systems around the world.

Included in this book are reflection pages for you to record your thoughts, emotions, ideas and any questions you may wish to ask those in your personal space, or the authors themselves.

IMPORTANT:

This book is NOT a replacement for professional help, and should you need help urgently we strongly advise you to reach out to the suicide prevention teams local to you, or the emergency services.

CONTENT WARNING:

This book includes topics such as rape, sex trafficking, domestic abuse, prostitution, body dysmorphia, drug and alcohol abuse, child abuse, violence and we advise you to take special care when reading, recommending or working with others using the contents of this book.

Liability:

The authors within this book, and the publisher, can in no way be held responsible for any negative outcomes following the reading of this book.

Today Was the Day My Light Ran Out.

Today was the day my light ran out, catching me unawares,
Leaving nothing left to give, not to you, not to me,
Not even to the shadows, lurking inside my mind.
You waltzed into my life, we talked, we laughed,
And bit by bit, you stole my light away,
Without us even realising it.
I'd opened the door, invited you in,
With a welcoming warmth, a beaming smile, kind words, encouragement and laughter.
It's only now I realise, I focused on serving others,
Forgetting to serve myself,
And now it's dark here, someone turned out the light.
You all came and took,
You gave a little, but took much more,
Staying a while, before you left,
Without a care,
Without a word.
It cut so deep,
And I wondered why,
Then the truth it came to pass,
That I had been the one, who'd given you all the key,
To the deepest, most sacred part of me.
You saw it, you touched it, used it,
And abused it,
And what is now left, is but an empty shell.
I look at the pills upon the side,

The knives and the rope I must hide.
The darkest thoughts, the darkest days,
These dangerous thoughts, they won't go away.
They lurk behind every corner,
Dancing the night away,
In my dreams, my waking moments,
Every God damned place I look.
But that's okay, you got what you came for,
Leaving me empty and broken, upon my kitchen floor.
I trusted you.
Opened up too soon,
And now I feel empty, alone and confused.
And as you walk your path,
Enjoying my light, wearing my smile, laughing my laugh,
You do not understand what is to come.
All I ask is you use them well,
Lighting the way, serving others,
Remembering as I should have done, to serve yourself too.
Take heed of my words,
Before those who surround you all disappear,
Because once the light goes out, there's no-one there.
You see they love the light, but not the dark,
Do not fear though,
A new and brighter light will grow,
From deep within the darkness,
From this sorrow I now bear,
And all you really stole, if truth be told,
Was the shedding of a skin, one which fits you perfectly,
For now, and for as long as you may need.

© Dawn Bates 2021

FOREWORD

According to Caroline Myss, American Author of Mysticism and Wellness, our goal as human beings is to transform ourselves. We long to attain power in the physical world, whilst also becoming beings who are empowered from within.

Although we have made significant progress in recent years to end the stigma surrounding mental health struggles, there is still a long way to go. We need to continue to debunk the myth that suicide is selfish, or a coward's way out. For myself and those I've met who share similar experiences the opposite remains the truth.

The human experience is messy and confusing, we are all winging it, and no-one has it easy. This compilation of moving personal stories, brings into sharp focus one of the more difficult places some of us have found ourselves in - the point of suicide.

Prepare to be inspired, empowered, and motivated. Find nuggets of gold to help you have a happier, healthier mind. Read practical advice that will give you new perspectives on how to make sense of our chaotic, beautiful, and perfectly imperfect lives.

From daily routines, such as meditation and journaling, to connecting with your spirituality and nourishing your soul. There's so much honest, powerful testimony to absorb written by honest, powerful women. They've all been there, done that and got the t-shirt - they know how it feels to be at rock bottom and want to show you how they survived so you can live your best life.

Debbie's rising mantra, 'I am possible' opens the endless potential of who we are and what we can achieve in the world. The power of her self-healing to become the incredible healer she now is, is uplifting - you can't beat the lived experience for empathy, understanding and evidence of how you can reclaim your strength. Her courage in putting these stories together, is a testament of how committed she is to helping others.

The book is packed with many wonderful ways to facilitate self-care. Debbie details her amazing mirror affirmations and breathing/visualisation exercises. Kim has some great steps to help reframe your mindset and understand that you are worth fighting for, every single day. Erica talks with gentleness and compassion about her inner child, knowing that to gain her trust, she must first trust herself - 'trust isn't about trusting other people, it's about trusting yourself.' She also offers some incredible sense-making of what it means to feel suicidal.

Melba has fantastic Thriving Tools from empathy towards others and self-forgiveness to allowing yourself to grieve. These tools can be used for all those things in life you will need to grieve - a person, a relationship, a job, your fertility, your childhood, your life before you began to thrive.

This book will help you understand what you can change and what you can't - what you need to work on and what you need to let go of. It will offer you a perspective of faith and spirituality, not only in the universe and your maker but also in yourself, your journey, and your purpose. We are not broken we just need to look inside of us for our answers to help us make sense of the world and our place in it.

Here is a book dedicated to highlighting our humanity and debunking the myths. It shows how we all share similar feelings, that we are not alone in how our emotions ebb and flow - that we have choice even when we can't see it. And that the hope for happiness in this life is still there, even when we think it isn't.

So, begin today by doing one small thing for yourself and then repeat it tomorrow and the next day. There's no quick fix to healing, the work is hard and through is always the way. There's also no right way to be, find what works for you and don't stop looking - these wounded healers all found their happy ending, what will your story be?

Penned by 'K'

Debbie Debonaire

Debbie Debonaire is an Emotional Resilience and Transformation Coach, Author, and Speaker. She is a mental Health Advocate and Suicide Prevention Campaigner as well as the founder and creator of HeartACT Approach. She has been a guest on several podcasts and radio shows, as well as a speaker on summits sharing her mission and message to make a difference in the world.

Debbie brings solutions, inspiration, and change, through her innovative process to guide career women (and men) from negative life patterns to triumphant transformation and empowerment. She has created a tool kit of resources from e-books to Mind Body Harmony video series on meditation and visualisations to help give people the courage to take back their control, and live life on their own terms so that they can thrive to their true potential with strengthened resilience to live the life they desire and deserve.

www.debbiedebonaire.com

The Storm Before the Calm

BY DEBBIE DEBONAIRE
UK

Have you ever had those moments when life just isn't worth living? Have you ever had those moments where you just deep down felt that your child would be much better off without you being in their life?

Have you ever been on the edge of the depths of darkness, where there is no way back?

Have you spiralled all the way down to the bottom?

Have you decided this is it, this is the time to go?

This is the time to relieve all of those around you, relieve some of the toxic life that you are creating.

Wait!

Let me take you back to when I was a little girl, age eight in primary school, happy go lucky. Not a care in the world, but at the age of eight, my world slowly began to cave in. I became the victim of a bully, and her entourage. Every night when the school bell rang. I ran and ran as fast as I could. Eyes darting everywhere, looking behind me, looking in front of me knowing that it didn't matter how far I ran, the bully would be there waiting for me underneath the underpass. There she was night after night, name-calling, hair pulling, prodding, poking, just horrendous for me whilst eight to ten other eight to nine-year-old girls stood there watching it all happen. The hair pulling, the throwing to the ground, the name-calling and the abuse went on and on and on. Until I became eleven years old and went to high school. Between the ages of eleven and thirteen, I had a wonderful, wonderful time, making new friends and adapting to becoming a teenager.

Then, at the age of thirteen, when the local high schools merged, back came the bully, and like a radar, she found me there in the corner of the schoolyard.

Once again, the taunting, the name-calling, the pushing, the shoving, throwing me to the ground, the hair-pulling all began again.

This carried on until the age of sixteen. The physical bullying and the mental abuse.

Why?

I never ever got to the bottom of the 'Why for her', but the 'Why me?' I discovered much later in life when I began reflecting on my victimhood mentality.

At the age of sixteen I left school, but I wasn't free. The mental abuse wasn't just at school.

It went on in my personal life too and had done so for many years previously. The taunting began with 'You're fat', 'You're stupid', 'You'll not amount to much', 'You're a mistake', 'You were a hole in a condom'.

These were the words as a young girl I heard on a regular basis, said to me by my dad when I was about eight, maybe ten years old

Even though I wanted to stay on at school, go to college and university to become a Primary School Teacher, I was told I had to go out to work, so I started my adult life as a shop assistant and on the first day of work, I met my future husband.

That first week of work was so much fun as we were preparing for the new shop to open and full of laughter, my escape from what was going on behind the scenes.

At the age of nineteen I got married and I thought the laughter would continue for years to come. Little did I realise I was jumping out of the proverbial frying pan into the fire. The mental bullying carried on year after year, after year, twenty-two of them in fact. 'You are not good enough', 'Who the hell do you think you are?', 'Get down off your pedestal?', 'I'm not a 'fucking' light switch you can turn on and off'.

I had to endure all the pressure of all the years of bullying, time after time, after time. Friends often used to say to me *'Why do you let him talk like that to you in public?'*

To be honest, I did not see it how they saw it. To me this was the norm, this was how I had been spoken to most of my life or maybe I did not want to admit. Even after the birth of my beautiful son they continued. The final straw came when I began to spiral to the edge of the depths of darkness, despair, and into the grasp of clinical depression.

You're either depressed or you're not depressed, or that's what I thought. I didn't realise clinical depression was an actual mental illness and an imbalance in the brain. Brilliant!

All the things I was taught as I was growing up "You're useless", "You will not amount to much", "You're thick", "Who do you think you are?" The mental illness proved them right, my brain was dysfunctional. I had a chemical imbalance and it spiralled out of control.

Then agoraphobia kicked in. I couldn't speak to people.

Lost, alone, not knowing what to do, where to go, who to speak to, spiralling into the depths of no return resulting in three attempted suicides. The last one, I should never have survived because I cut the brakes on my car and drove it at high speed into a wall. For whatever reason, I did survive and that started the journey back from the depths of despair. I started the journey out of the darkness that had been my life for so long.

It was a struggle, an almighty struggle. I reached out to someone who I believed could help me, and give them credit, they did get me a certain part of the way.

Then history repeated itself as the person crossed over the professional boundary line and found feelings for me. They began to control me, started to blame me and tell me it was all my fault. They said we couldn't carry on like this, we had to end the relationship. But we didn't have a relationship, or did we? Not in my mind we didn't.

All this time when I was going through my clinical depression, my little boy, at the age of five, witnessed a mum who was out of control with agoraphobia. He had to hold my hand to get me out of the house and into the car. I was constantly trying to hide the fact that I had been crying or tried to self-harm.

However hard I believed I was trying to hide everything from him, I believed I was a toxic person in his life because I was told I was an unfit mother and that he would be better off without me.

Words I heard repeatedly from his dad, and that toxicity was the reason I kept telling myself I needed to be out of his life. I didn't care about anyone else, not my husband or my own extended family.

But I did care. I cared very deeply about each one of them, especially my son. I cared for them so much that I truly believed the best thing for me to do was not have a place on this earth.

I tried three times to remove the toxicity I believed I was full of from all their lives.

THE BEAUTY OF WATER

Walking has always been a passion of mine. Every opportunity I could get I would go for a walk, in my school days and beyond. The outdoors was my saviour, my escape. Camping, trekking, hiking, canoeing, they all gave me a sense of peace, freedom and happiness.

A feeling of being alive in the depths of clinical depression and in times of living in a relationship of infidelity, which became apparent after seven years of our marriage, but which I chose to ignore because I couldn't prove it at the time, I only found evidence much later in our marriage.

Walking allowed me to think, allowed my mind to wonder and it is on one of these particular walks that my mind wandered to a very dark place and I carried out my first suicide failure.

I had left home feeling broken and despairing yet again, being told I was worthless and an unfit mother. As I began to walk my mind was racing, I was so engrossed in the turmoil in my mind that I was oblivious as to where I was walking, until I found myself standing on a bridge overlooking the canal.

The water was so inviting, reaching out to me, telling me it could take the pain away. Its depths could take my hurt away, its power could wash over me cleaning away the toxicity of my soul and carry me to a blissful place. A place where I would be safe, having set my son free. Free of the toxicity I was showering down on him.

I don't remember climbing over the barrier, all I remember is the breeze sweeping over my body as I floated through the air in what felt like slow motion on my descent and the splash of the water as my body entered the water. I have a vision of me lying on the bed of the canal, lifeless and at peace.

Then, I was spluttering and lashing out my arms at someone. I did not know him but this man with dark hair, a round face and dark features, saved me, and I do not even remember his name. I am not sure how long I lay on the bank of the canal or how long the man had been with me. All I kept screaming at him was "No! No!". He kept saying he should call for an ambulance. However, for whatever reason he didn't.

The next thing I remember is this man walking with me along my street. It was such a strange feeling. I was walking, but I didn't feel like I was fully aware of what was going on, like I was watching myself from the outside in. It was all just a blur. Somehow, he had my house keys in his hand and put the key in the lock.

I woke up the next day as if the previous day had not happened. The only reminders were the wet clothes in a pile on the floor, bruises and grazes on my hands, arms and legs and a very swollen, painful ankle which I had obviously received, landing in the bottom of the canal.

The man was gone, and I never saw him again. I am not sure how I kept the bruises or grazes and the events of that day hidden from my husband or my son, but nothing was ever mentioned.

As I reflected sometime later in my life, it may have been a time when my husband was working away from home, but I have no recollection of how I kept it from my son. Furthermore, I always wondered why this man took me home and did not insist on taking me to the hospital. I had in the back of my mind that maybe it had been my ex-husband

A BITTER/SWEET PILL

Suicide failure number two was one I regretted for quite a long time, the regret was not the failure itself, but the time and the place I carried it out. When you are in the zone of suicidal thoughts, nothing is rational or sensible to those on the outside, and certainly not for me on the inside reflecting on things. At the time I believed I knew exactly what I was doing and why I was doing it. What wasn't present in these thoughts was where I was or who I was with.

You see, because of my passion for the outdoors, I became a cub scout leader known as Raksha (Mowgli's adopted wolf mum in Rudyard Kipling's Jungle Book). It was whilst I was on one of our many organised cub camps that my thoughts and urges to leave my life took over me.

I always carried lots of painkillers with me for back problems I was enduring at the time. Suicidal thoughts can mix up the logical with the illogical, and on this occasion that's exactly what happened. The feelings of wanting to take an overdose were very powerful that day. I was engulfed by them but at the same time was able to carry out my duties of the day fluently and with no 'hiccups'.

It wasn't until we all retired for the night that the urge got so great it took over me. I took myself off to my car in the car park with pills and water bottle in hand and proceeded to sit in my car and carry out the act in the pitch darkness.

I had no recollection of what time it was or how long I had been there as I blacked out at some point during this attempt. The next thing I can vaguely remember, I say vaguely because my vision was blurred, was being carried and someone speaking to me, then staring at the ceiling of an ambulance. I opened my eyes and realised I was staring at a different ceiling. I was in a hospital bed feeling very groggy, with a very sore throat, headache and feeling very weak.

I'd failed again! Anger. Disappointment. Frustration. I felt them all and more besides, with all-consuming tears, and goodness there were lots of tears.

I also managed to keep this episode from my family too. Neither were part of the trip and when I was discharged from the hospital, one of the other leaders who had stayed with me took me back to the basecamp to pick up my things.

When we got there, my tent had been taken down, my car was packed and I drove home with the other cub-leader who had initially found me, a necessity to make sure I got there safely.

Thankfully, none of the children saw what had happened. I was interviewed by the Chief Scout about a week after and it was decided that I could stay as a cub leader but was never allowed to go on future cub camps.

WHAT? NO BRAKES?

My final suicide failure came towards the end of my marriage, I say towards the end, but it had been on the rocks for some time. I had decided I wanted to get away for a week in a cottage in the country by myself, to see if I would miss my husband. I wanted to know what feelings I still had for him, if any, and what to do regarding my marriage, having found photos and emails from 'A.N. Other Woman' or women.

I do not know to this day if there was one, two or many. The day came for me to leave for my trip and what happened prior to me leaving will always stay with me.

I brought my suitcase down, packed everything into my car and then sat on the sofa with my son who was only about eight at the time and I gave him lots of hugs and kisses to say goodbye and wished him a lovely time spending boy time together with his daddy.

Unfortunately, as his daddy stood and watched, my son became hysterical and wouldn't get off my knee. He begged and pleaded with me not to go and virtually pinned me to the sofa. I looked up to my then husband for help and support and he just stood there and shrugged his shoulders.

What I did next, I did not forgive myself for in a very long time. I prized my son's arms from around my neck, gave him a huge kiss, told him how much I loved him and with tears running down his face and mine I walked out of the house, got into my car, and drove away.

Now you would have thought that this episode should have instilled in me how much my little boy needed me but no, all I could hear ringing in my ears as I drove away was 'You're an unfit mother'

'Useless'

'Worthless'

'You will never amount to much'

Constantly throbbing in my head as I journeyed the one hundred and fifty miles to my destination.

For the first four days, I binged on a bottle of Gin and Tonic and a box of Lindor Chocolates per day. For someone who did not drink much that was scary, but at the same time it eased the pain. Only a couple of my friends knew where I was and for days I would respond to their texts and then slowly as the days went on, I would reply only once. I spent most nights reflecting, realising I had no more love left in me for my husband and my marriage was a sham. No matter how hard I tried to bring the good memories up, yes there were many, they were overshadowed by the taunting and the mental abuse.

I walked for miles that week asking Mother Nature for the answers, but with the constant Gin and Tonic fog, and negative blockbuster playing in my head, I could not see her guidance, or hear what she was trying to say to me. It all got too much, and the suicidal thoughts returned strengthened by 'I am the toxic person in my son's life'

'My son is better off without me'

'I am an unfit mother'

'He would have a better life without me in it'

That night, I planned it all, and with no idea where the plan came from I went to my car and like a woman possessed I made sure I disabled the brakes. Immediately I felt so calm and in control, the logic and illogical at play again, having a merry dance. I got into the car and drove it as fast as I could into a dry-stone wall. I remember as I got ever closer and closer to the wall I shouted "You're Free Adam! You're FREE!'

Then everything went black.

Coming into view was a bright white light, I had made it! Here was the bright white light people talk about seeing when passing over from one world to the next, from life into death.

I felt so at peace, but the peace was about to be shattered because this bright light was not what I thought it was. You see, I had not driven fast enough, I had not driven hard enough, I had not smashed hard enough into the wall and the bright white light was shining down on me from the ceiling lights as I lay in a hospital bed.

Voices surrounded me, twittering bouncing off the walls. I had failed again.

I let out an almighty scream, went into an uncontrollable rage. I was so angry that I had failed again, so angry that I had not rid my son of the toxicity in his life again!

In the years that followed I realised the reason I had been saved each time. The reasons why suicide is not the answer.

MY 'OH SHIT' MOMENT

The next few weeks and months were so hard for me, struggling to be there for my son, struggling because the marriage had ended, struggling because I did not want to hurt my little boy again. How can I become a fit mother when I was broken into so many pieces?

It wasn't until sometime later I realised why I had been saved.

The thing that got me on my true journey to recovery was one night in bed. I woke up with an empty red wine bottle in my hand in bed alone. The ex-husband was gone, my little boy was asleep in his room next door, and as I looked down at that empty red wine bottle. I thought, "Oh shit! Adam is next door, asleep! He could come in here and find me in this mess!"

And that is when it happened. Call it an hallucination, a sixth sense, imagination. Call it what the hell you want, but I saw my little boy's face right in front of me, right there in front of my own face. The expression on that face and the tears in those eyes were the thing that gave me the reason to climb fully out of the darkness.

It took me a long time, six years in fact, but I did come out of the end of that tunnel. That" Oh shit!" moment, my little boy's face in front of me, they changed my life for the better. I've worked damn hard on myself to create the person I am today. Yes, there were lots of ups and downs. Lots of them.

I've turned those adversities into triumphs and at the age of forty-seven, I gained a first-class honours degree. Me the thick one! Who the hell did I think I was? Getting down off my pedestal with a first-class honour's degree! Wow!

Then, in 2012, I completed a twelve-day Inca Trail trek raising three and a half thousand pounds for a children's disability charity. Despite, on the first day, falling and damaging my leg, which later transpired into a full-on hip replacement surgery! (Yes, I am the bionic woman! LOL!) I carried on, not just for me but for all those children who would benefit from me getting to the end.

What pushed me on was that little face that I saw that night moving me forward, pushing me forward, getting me to the end, making me realise how I was worth something. Since then, it's also made me realise that I do have a bloody purpose on this earth. My purpose on this earth is to reach out to as many women (and men) as I possibly can who find themselves on the edges of the depths of despair.

My purpose is to guide inspire, empower, encourage them into transforming themselves so that they can live the life they love and find their true freedom to: -

'Choose LIFE! Choose FREEDOM! Choose YOU!' Just as I have done.

Our life is our stage, whatever has happened so far. Good or bad, we have the power within us to rewrite the script of our lives, especially if the future life ahead of us is not appearing in the spotlight as we would like it to. As a woman who has lost control in certain areas of her life, take it from me, you can live the life you want to live on your terms, under your control, and you can thrive.

THE JOURNEY OF TRANSFORMATION

Going on a transformational journey I found myself going through a jungle of emotions as I worked on loving the person inside of me. Loving the young child that I used to believe I had failed was tough going.

As I worked on each aspect of my transformation, I was able to take steps towards getting out of the jungle, facing the trees that blocked my path. The animals, aka the bullies, who continued to control the direction I was trying to go in still had power over me; until I saw the opening and stepped forward into a meadow. I had set myself free and now allowed myself to make my own choices.

I removed the mask which I had hidden behind most of my life. I chose my own direction, and I created the life stage I am proud to stand on, with the spotlight I love to shine in.

Many times, I have rewritten my life script, refocused the plot, reset the scenes so I could step into the Director and Leading Lady of my life, the life I was born to live, achieving all I desired (and deserved) and had set my heart on. Not an easy show to perform, but all the rehearsals have been worth all the blood sweat and tears.

I now look forward to the next set of rehearsals, the next scenes to plan where I am thriving in a life that nearly did not happen.

However, life is not a rehearsal, is it? Every moment of every day, our life needs to be fulfilled. We only have each moment that we stand in once, and then it is gone.

So, what happened during the transformation that kept me pushing forward? The main motivation was the vision I mentioned earlier, the life I wanted to give my son, the life he deserved, the life we deserved. I knew I had to work on myself and knew I had to find myself. I had to reach deep inside of me to find the person I was truly born to be, so I embarked on a six-year journey of personal development finding out who I truly was.

Starting with stepping in front of the mirror having not done so for 9 years, to tell this woman staring back at me how much I love her. Staring into her eyes, going deep into her heart showing her the sincerity of my love for her.

This was a huge step that I took in the beginning of my transformational journey and one I continue to do today. It was a very difficult part of the journey because for many days I just got up and walked in front of the mirror, and with my eyes shut I stood there for a few moments before walking away, without opening my eyes, just simply going through the motions.

Then one day I opened my eyes, looked into the mirror, and looked at the woman staring back at me. It was the start of a journey that was beautiful and traumatic all at the same time. I didn't just see a woman in the mirror, I saw a beautiful soul, and whilst staring into her eyes and getting deep into her heart, I told her how much I loved her just the way she was. I was then on a mission to be constantly striving forward to be able to bring her out to the surface, to show her what life was really like, and not the life that she had endured.

Once I found my true self, I wanted more, I wanted to learn more, I wanted to know how to say 'No', I wanted to know how to make my own choices and decisions. No easy feat I can tell you, especially when imposter syndrome struck. It would send me back a few steps until I no longer feared it, but I chose to look at it squarely in the face and told it that it had no space in my life.

I discovered affirmations and proclamations, meditation, the Law of Attraction, Quantum Physics and one's own energy and auras. Some of which I am still finding out about as I delve deeper into being of full service to others.

I have a gratitude journal which I write in daily sharing with the Universe all the things I am grateful for. I also have a deep diving journal which I use when I feel out of alignment so that I can find out what is pulling or pushing me sideways, as well as an everyday journal which I use to reflect on my day each evening before I go to bed.

I stepped into self-love and self-care like they were going out of fashion, and I needed to find out everything about them before it was too late. With these techniques and strategies, I allowed myself, and continue to allow myself 'me' time. I created a morning routine that has developed over the years. A monthly full-on self-care and self-love Sunday where I create my own home spa and really pamper myself.

I began to listen to my body, my heart, and my mind, to see what was going on for me so that I could see what needed to change for my life to move forward every day. I began to listen to the language I was using, realising lots needed to change because of the language that had been used for me in the past.

The negative language was not serving me now, nor did it ever. This was mind blowing and I used to have a language journal in which I would write down all the negative language I used, helping me discover a positive opposite language I could promote in my life instead. To be honest, I still must check in with myself from time to time when things are not flowing as it can still trip me up.

Yes, I have achieved a lot since I lived my victimhood lifestyle, and yet there is still so much more to achieve, always something new to try, something new to learn that makes life exciting.

The path I was on was a difficult one with lots of ups and downs but the undying love I have for my son always kept me going. What keeps me ever thriving forward today is the love I have for myself as well as my son.

I have love for those who have lost their way looking for guidance, and I have love for those who guide others in overcoming adversities and challenges.

Every day I celebrate life, my life and the life of others who are striving on their own journey of transformation, finding their true calling. If you would have told me many years prior that I would have accomplished so much in my life so far, I would not have believed you.

We are forever transforming when we live our life to the fullest. My biggest transformation period was between the ages of forty-five and fifty, lifting up a first-class honours degree at the age of forty-seven, raising £3500 for a children's disability charity by conquering a twelve-day trek of the Inca Trail in Peru - an amazing life experience which has been a dream of mine since I was twelve years old when I studied the Incas in high school.

Four years after the Inca Trail, and my hip replacement operation, I researched the relationship between the brain and the heart. I learnt how the mind and the soul interlink to either make us or break us, depending on how we wire our system. I became fascinated in how thoughts and emotions are related and transmitted, finding out that the heart sends more information to the brain than the other way around.

Find out our feelings are what trigger our thoughts and not necessarily the other way round, the dynamic of this relationship, gave me further enlightenment.

When I put it into action guiding others how if we change our emotions towards something or someone, we can change our thoughts and rewrite our life script. The whole approach uncovered my empathy and altruism to embarked on a holistic counselling course, and in 2016 I qualified as a Holistic Counsellor Meditation Teacher, and a Human Developer specialising in building and strengthening resilience. I studied and qualified in Trauma Therapy and other modalities including Cognitive Behavioural Therapy. These enabled me to move people forward in their lives and changed the course of my life to step onto my own life stage where I could perform my life's passion and purpose from which HeartACT™ was born. To guide, empower and inspire others to take back control and live life on their own terms.

This journey has been amazing, once I removed the shiny object syndrome which involved countless guru's promising that what they had to offer would change my life. I followed my heart to serve the world. Once I did that, I opened doors for myself and I have met amazing men and women, who like me want to make a difference in this world. I have met and I am still meeting men and women who are changing their lives around and coming to me for guidance to find their freedom so that they can take back their control and live life on their terms.

I filled the missing piece of the HeartACT™ puzzle by qualifying as a HeartMath™ Coach. I now run my own business as an Emotional Resilience Consultant and Transformation Coach. I am free from the control of others, and I have created a community movement which continues to grow, fulfilling my mission of making a difference to 10,000 people's lives. I use the HeartACT Approach, which takes people from where they are now in their current life so that they too can step into a life in which to thrive.

I have fulfilled another dream of becoming an author, and have written two books, whilst being the curator and one of the authors in this powerful anthology of inspiring stories. This book was born out of a dream I had five years ago to write a book called a 'Alive to Thrive' bringing together ten women, including myself, to share their stories of overcoming challenges and adversities, failing suicide and striving in life; and if I can do this, then there is hope for all of us to achieve our dreams.

TAKING DIFFERENT DIRECTIONS AND BUILDING MY SCENERY

The following are tips, strategies, and techniques that I have learnt to use on myself, and have further developed, to implement with my clients today.

The Art of Mindful Re-shaping

Mindful Re-shaping is the name I give to deliberately altering your state or circumstances. It's a form of meditation, but I would love for you to know that you are in control, so Mindful Re-shaping is a very useful tool, whenever you are in crisis, overwhelmed, panic, or you feel de-stabilised in any way.

Mindful Re-shaping begins with your breathing to take you into a state of alert mindfulness. This is the most powerful freedom of thought!

Observing your own breathing, listening to your breath as you breathe in and out, in and out, in and out, allows you to change your state, by changing how you are breathing, the shallow breathing of anxiety can be slowed and quieted as you are in control of it when you take time to become aware of it. The simplest way to slow your breathing down, is to count as you breathe

For those who have not done breathwork before, here is an introduction:

Breathe in for the count of three, hold for the count of three, breathe out for the count of 3.

When you have controlled your breathing to this level then up the count to five for each step. This will slow down your breathing, calm your panic and overwhelm and stabilise you.

This is one of many breathing techniques I use from my toolkit.

The Art of Conscious Concentration

When you are in the flow of conscious concentration, you are better equipped to control your thoughts in the future. Conscious concentration involves focusing on a single point. For instance, repeating a single word or mantra of your choice. You could try concentrating on a candle flame, listening to a single gong, or counting beads on your rosary.

The objective is on focusing the mind on absolute presence, and in doing so, will encourage the thought re-shaping to take place. You only need to do this exercise for a few moments in the beginning. Build upon each time with a longer duration, to an optimal time you feel the need to reach in order to relax your body and mind to prepare you to be in the state of grace that will enhance the rest of the day.

The intention of these two exercises is not to get involved in your thoughts or to judge them, but simply to be aware of each mental activity as it arises. Through Mindful Re-shaping, and Conscious Concentration you can see how your thoughts and feelings tend to move in a particular pattern. Over time you become more aware of your own human tendencies and therefore can take control and change.

As you practice you will help yourself to create an inner balance which will bring you into your true alignment. Using these two techniques gives you a starting point to be able to relax your mind, body, and soul, when you are in a stressful situation or an uncomfortable circumstance.

Being able to re-frame your thoughts and bring yourself to a centred state, rewards you with a clearer and more neutral mood, to carry on through the rest of your day and the continuation of your own personal journey. The instantly calming sequences of Conscious Concentration and Mindful Re-shaping are great when you have enough control over your time to enjoy them.

But we sometimes need skills and reflexes that will assist us in a crisis that requires more urgent action. Here is a six-step program that minimizes the negative effects of stress the moment the body begins its fight-or-flight reaction.

Instant Calming Sequence

Step 1: Practice uninterrupted breathing and Mindful Re-shaping.

When acute stress strikes, immediately focus on your breathing and continue breathing smoothly, deeply, and evenly.

Step 2: Put on a positive face, even if you don't feel like it. Smile a grin that you can feel in the corners of your eyes. The conventional wisdom is that happiness triggers smiling. Recent studies suggest that this process works the other way. Smiling can raise your endorphins, and in stressful situations, it can help keep you calm. Try this simple test: Smile a broad grin right now. Look in the mirror if you have one! Don't you feel better already?

Step 3: Balance your posture. People under stress often look hunched-over, hence the often-repeated phrase, "They have the weight of the world on their shoulders." Maintaining good posture works like smiling, "Physical balance contributes to emotional balance." Keep your head up, chin-in, chest high, pelvis and hips level, back comfortably straight and abdomen free of tension. Imagine a sky hook lifting your body from a point at the centre of the top of your head.

Step 4: Close your eyes and imagine somewhere idyllic. Imagine, for example, you're standing under a warm, fragrant waterfall that washes away all your tension. Feel it's purifying effect, soothing tension, and frustration. Or imagine you're lying in a sunny meadow field on a soft blanket. Smell the wildflowers and feel the breeze on your skin.

Step 5: Acknowledge reality. Face your causes of stress head-on. Don't try to deny it or wish that it hadn't happened. Think: "This is real. I can handle it. I'm finding the best possible way to cope right now."

Step 6: Reassert control. Instead of fretting about how the stressor has robbed you of control, focus on what you can control and take appropriate action.

Quick Mantra Meditation

Step 1: Sit in a comfortable position (always make sure your spine is straight).

Step 2: Choose a word or short phrase to focus on that feels connected to your personal belief system. A non-religious person might choose a word like peace or love. Some might use a favourite line from a prayer from their religion

Step 3: Close your eyes. ·

Step 4: Scan through your body and relax all your muscles from head to toes (Tensing the muscles briefly before relaxing them). ·

Step 5: Then just breathe slowly and naturally while repeating your chosen word or phrase in your mind as you exhale.

Step 6: When other thoughts come into your mind, simply acknowledge that you are thinking and gently refocus on repeating your mantra.

Step 7: Do this for ten to twenty minutes. It is ok to open your eyes occasionally to check the time if you need to, but it is best not to use an alarm. ·

Step 8: When you have finished, sit quietly for a minute or so with your eyes closed and then relax for a minute with your eyes open. Remain seated for at least one or two minutes.

Step 9: Plan for a session once or twice a day.

Reclaiming Your Self-Esteem Guided Visualisation

Begin by getting into a comfortable position whether that is lying down or sitting in a comfortable chair. Now close your eyes and concentrate on your breathing, begin to slowly breathe out and then slowly breathe in. Repeat this until you feel yourself relaxing. Now imagine yourself slowly walking along a sandy beach or by the banks of a river or along the side of a lake whatever resonates with you best. As you walk along, become aware of all your senses, taste, sight, smell, sound, touch. As you become aware of each one, take a few moments to be present with them. When you are ready, start to walk towards the water's edge, when you reach it slowly look into the water at your reflection, what do you see?

Take a moment, look at your reflection. As you look at your reflection, I want you to become aware of your breathing again, breathe out slowly then breathe in slowly until all your attention is on your breathing. When you are ready, come back into the room and begin this technique.

To start, stand in front of your mirror and look at the fabulous person looking back at you. Smile and say to the person in the mirror, (insert whatever your name is), followed by, "I love you unconditionally," or you can say, "I love you, (insert whatever your name is) unconditionally." Then, repeat the following whilst still looking at the fabulous person in the mirror. "I accept myself just the way I am.

Repeat that ten times first thing when you get out of bed in the morning, this will get you positioned mentally, in a better place for the rest of the day.

Carry out these techniques daily. I appreciate that it may be difficult at first. But be persistent with the process. When you can reclaim your self-esteem, you are able to feel more confident about yourself.

I would like to give thanks and gratitude to the lady who taught and inspired me to become a Holistic Counsellor Dr Christine Cunningham from the Institute of Meditation Teacher Training Association.

HEARTACT APPROACH™ THEATRAPY™

Life Stage Directions

Prologue - establishing current self
In order to move forward we need to understand the place, we are currently at.
- ✓ **T**he plot and storyline - how do you want your life to unfold
- ✓ **H**arnessing your life script - creating your life story
- ✓ **E**stablishing your scenes - what do you want to achieve in your daily life
- ✓ **A**cknowledging the characters - who is in your life space
- ✓ **T**erminating the properties - finding what is holding you back
- ✓ **R**eplacing the entrances and exits - looking at where you want to go in life
- ✓ **A**bolishing the rehearsals - stop procrastination, changing the perspectives
- ✓ **P**reparing the finale - planning your true purpose in life
- ✓ **Y**our true self - you as the leading lady/man in your own life.

The Finale - Stepping out of your comfort zone to live your newfound life to the fullest as you CHOOSE LIFE CHOOSE FREEDOM CHOOSE YOU

With heartfelt love, appreciation, and resilience,
Debbie

If you, or you suspect a loved one, friend or colleague are dealing with mental health challenges and need support then reach out to me or any of the authors in this book to guide you.

You can find me here **https://www.heartact.co.uk**

REFLECTIONS

REFLECTIONS

REFLECTIONS

Dawn Bates

Dawn Bates is a true international bestselling author multiple times over on 5 continents. She specialises in developing AUTHORities who wish to give a voice to the voiceless whilst working with them to create brand expansion strategies through activism, authorship, and business.

With social justice and human rights underpinning everything she does, including her study with the University of Oxford where she is working towards for her PhD in Human Rights and Social Justice, you can guarantee her books are powerful.

Dawn brings together the multi-faceted aspects of the world we live in and takes you on a rollercoaster ride of joy and inspiration, whilst delivering mic dropping insights, motivation and awakening. Her work captures life around the world in all its rawness.

To discover more about Dawn, please visit
www.dawnbates.com

More Than My Name

BY DAWN BATES
LOCATION FREE

My head felt heavy, my mouth was dry, and my body felt as if it wasn't there. As I turned my head to the right and looked towards the window, I saw my dad sat on a chair by the foot of my bed. He had one of his fishing magazines in his hands and as soon as he heard me move, he looked up. He never did that. Once his head was in one of his fishing magazines, he was like me with my head in a book - nothing could distract us.

The look of concern on his face confused me, and what was he doing in my room anyway?

I tried to move, but I just didn't have the energy or the strength, and my head was pounding. Nausea swept over me, and I really needed a drink of water. Dad got up from his chair and looked down at me and said "Well that was a bloody silly thing to do, you silly sod. What did you do that for?".

The tears fell and I didn't even know why I was crying, but it was the look of concern and love he had for me that made me cry. I had never seen him look at me like that before. A mixture of love, fear, fierce protection with sadness and a hint of anger. He lifted me up so I could drink and then passed me the glass of water from the chest of drawers.

I could hear the emotion in his voice. "You had us all worried, your mum's worried sick, and I'm not best pleased. Don't you ever go doing anything like that again, you hear me?" Stroking back my hair and asking if I wanted anything else, I felt more love from him than I had ever done. I really did feel like Daddy's little girl, something I hadn't felt with my dad until now.

As the moments passed, I had flashbacks of the hospital: the nasty taste in my mouth, the oxygen mask over my face and the drips in my arm. Other girls laying in their beds around me and doctors and nurses looking at my notes, taking my blood pressure, writing something down, and then walking away. All the images swimming around in my head, making me feel nauseous.

Then I remembered the vodka, mum's co-codamol and the tears. I had failed them all. I hadn't got the grades I wanted and needed to be able to take care of us all. It was my job to make sure we were all taken care of when mum and dad were too old to do so. I had to be the smartest of us all.

I had studied so hard, hidden from the bullies, hidden the bruises and the bumps on my head from where it had been smacked up against the brick walls at school, and yet I had still failed them all. I was eating food and then throwing it up doing my best not to get fat, all whilst there were people starving in the world.

How selfish could I be?

Thinking back now, this was far too much guilt and shame to carry on my young shoulders.

I was fifteen.

I'd just found out the man who was my biological father was a transvestite and not a 'proper' man.

He didn't love me and had told mum that he'd rather give me up for adoption to my new dad rather than pay another penny towards me and my education.

I'd also just been raped for the first time by a 'good Christian man who couldn't possibly hurt anyone'.

Mum and dad didn't know. How could I tell them when I'd told my friend the morning after what he'd done, and she hadn't believed me?

She said she'd heard me crying, had heard me in the shower afterwards, and yet hadn't gotten out of bed to come and see if I was okay. She said I was just making it up, just teasing him because I knew he liked me and just because I kept saying no, I didn't mean it. How could I mean it? He was a nice guy; someone other girls would kill to have as a boyfriend. What was wrong me?

Yeah, what was wrong with me?

Why did I keep getting bullied?

Why did I eat and then purge?

Why hadn't I got more than a B, C, or a D in my mock exams?

Why didn't my father want me?

Why wasn't he a proper man, one who provided for his family, the family he had created and just quit on? Why did he have to wear women's clothes? What was wrong with him? Men weren't supposed to wear women's clothes. Men weren't supposed to have long nails or shave their legs. Men were supposed to be men, wear men's clothes, have callused hands and do whatever it took to provide for their wife and children.

The weight of it all had gotten to be too much for me, and I wanted to stop the pain, the tears and loneliness. My brother didn't want me around and neither did my sister. Mum kept telling me that she loved me but didn't like me very much, so what was the point in living? I would miss my books, and my dog, but then again, I would be dead so wouldn't miss anything. No one wanted me so no one would miss me.

I'd taken the bottle of Vodka from the back of the cupboard, a bottle left over from a Christmas Day years ago because mum and dad didn't drink, well other than a 'hot toddy' for mum if she were on the rare occasion sick and the occasional Vodka and Orange at Christmas for dad.

I'd gone through the medicine cabinet and found mum's new prescription for her pain killers for her slipped disc. I took just enough so she would still have some in case she was in pain.

Going back to my bedroom with the vodka and the pills, followed by my dog Patsy, I was crying. Sitting on the end of my bed I took the lot. I didn't bother with a note and gave my dog Patsy a big hug and told her

I loved her. She kept trying to get in the way of what was happening, like she knew what I was doing, but I carried on until all pills were gone. The smell of the Vodka made me feel sick, and combined with the pills, I kept gagging.

I don't remember much more, other than what I've described above. Dad told me that I'd been asleep for a good eighteen hours and been in hospital for a few days. It had been too late to pump my stomach and so they'd flushed my system, whatever that meant.

Apparently, I'd been one of the lucky ones.

Looking at my dad, I remember my eyelids feeling heavy and then waking up to see my mum sat where dad had been sitting. It was an around the clock vigil to make sure I was okay, or was it to make sure I didn't attempt it again? I didn't see my brother or my sister, even though my sister and I shared a room.

Mum looked so tired, and the guilt swept over me. How could I have done what I'd done, putting mum and dad through this? How selfish of me! I remember trying to say "I'm sorry Mum" but my mouth was so dry I couldn't say anything. I just remember sitting there looking at her, looking at me.

I remember her saying to me "You silly sod" and trying to laugh because that is exactly what dad had said, but all that came out was a kind of cough. The fear filled my mum's face and she rushed to my side shouting "Roger!"

Dad was there in an instant, and mum was crying. Dad helped me sit up and mum put a damp cloth to my lips to wet them "to stop the cold sores" mum had said "because you look rough enough without adding to it". She always knew how to make you feel better in a bizarre twist of words.

The next thing I remember I was sat up in bed with Patsy at my feet and a book lying beside me and an intense hunger. All I could think about was Shepherd's Pie, carrots, green beans, and onion gravy, with roast potatoes. I got up out of bed and it took me ages to stand up and walk. I felt as though I hadn't moved in ages my body felt so stiff. Patsy jumped down, went to the top of the stairs, and barked. Mum was up the stairs in no time at all, with my dad close behind her. "I'm hungry, what's for dinner?" I asked my mum, and she said "Your favourite, Shepherd's Pie, carrots, beans, and roast potatoes with onion gravy. It will be ready in about half an hour. You coming down for a cup of tea?". I remember smiling at the thought of a cup of tea, in my bone China cup: the only way to really drink tea.

As the days passed by mum told me it had been dad who had found me in bed almost choking on my own vomit. He had tried to help me down to the bathroom when he heard the knock of the empty vodka bottle against the wooden post of my bed and the rustle of the pill packets in my dressing gown pocket. It was him who'd taken me downstairs and called the ambulance. I had no memory of it then, and no memory of it now.

When I told mum why I'd done what I'd done, she cried and told me that she didn't liked me very much because I was a lot like her and would argue the bloody point all the time. I was also bloody stubborn which clashed with her own personality. As for my father, I wasn't to worry about him anymore, even though she knew it would be hard. The next on the 'list' was my grades which 'For heaven's sake Dawn Louise! Grades are not the be all and end all of life; and what the hell was wrong with the grades anyway? They were better than the rest of them had ever got; and it wasn't my job to take care of anyone other than myself."

I didn't mention being raped, but she must have known because the Yellow Pages came out a few nights later with the pages open at abortion clinics "if it was needed".

I devoured the Shepherd's pie, and then asked for more, but there wasn't any. There was however apple crumble and custard, my other favourite. I was being spoilt and I joked that maybe I should do it again if I was going to get all my favourite foods, to which my mum threw me a fierce look whilst stating very firmly "If you ever try that again, I'll kill you my-bloody-self young lady!" with my dad adding "You ever upset your mother like that again, I'll be behind her next in line to put my foot up your arse!".

I hung my head in shame, and realised my sense of humour wasn't for them, even though it was my way of breaking the tension. I found out my brother and sister had been staying at Nanny and Grandad's and had been eating all my favourite treacle tarts and custard.

As the days and weeks passed nothing was ever mentioned about what I'd done, and it was soon as if nothing had ever happened. I threw myself into my study as it was one way to distract myself from the pain I felt in my heart about my father's rejection and what 'the good Christian boy' had done.

If I worked hard enough, I didn't feel anything because I didn't have time to think about either event. I got all higher grades, not As, mostly Bs, with two Cs, one for Maths and the other for Humanities with two Ds for science.

I got the grades I needed for college and continued to numb the pain I was feeling by going raving at weekends taking drugs. I got caught up with a very wrong crowd and I remember one time going so far into the world of drugs that seeing a big duffle bag filled with bundles of cannabis, base amphetamines, bags of hundreds of ecstasy tablets and bricks of cocaine in front of me and it not registering as a problem.

It had become normal that this lot would turn up and Thursday nights would mean stripping to my undies whilst bagging up pills, cutting up amphetamines with glucose and putting the mix, as well as the cocaine into 1gm wraps for Friday and Saturday night parties. There came a point where I'd been awake for three weeks totally off my face and had not even been to lectures or called home. My friends and family had been really worried, but I was too far gone to even care or realise, until a friend Matt looked at me in disgust when I walked up to him outside the common room at college. He told me to go and take a good hard look at myself, because he could no longer be friends with me if I was going to keep on the path I was on. Shock ripped through me and I remember frowning and then heading off to the park to lie down in the sun to think about what he'd said.

Matt's words were the wakeup call I needed, and I started to get my act together. I broke it off with the guy I was seeing and started pouring my efforts into my study. I had a lot to catch up on and catch up I did, and not just on my college work, but on the missed meals and lost weight. I stopped hanging out with the people from before and managed to avoid them in the raves I went to. I couldn't stop going to the raves, the techno music spoke to me on so many levels, as did the trance music.

The clearer my head, the more lost in the music and my own world I became, and the better the dancer I was. The better the dancer, the more attention I got, and the more I retreated into my own world. Having always been lost in the world of books, I now had another outlet of escape, the music, and the dancefloor.

The further I started to retreat into myself, the more ideas I had, and the happier I was. My books and the dancefloor never hurt me, never rejected me, and never betrayed me. They were my safety net, and later in life they would become my springboard.

Gaining the confidence to lose myself on the dancefloor, just being lost in the moment meant I wanted less and less drugs. I wanted to dance without them. I wanted to reach those highs of drugs naturally.

I started running, and started swimming more, and then I noticed a pattern. The more on my own I was, the happier I was. Lost in the world of books learning about the world itself, the how, the why, the when, and the who.

Lost in make believe worlds imagining all kinds of lives I could live, and then whilst swimming, running, and dancing I would move the pain and the sense of loss, guilt and shame out of my body.

I would go for long walks, without a word to anyone just to clear my mind. I remember one time my mum and dad were so worried about me because I'd been gone for hours. I had walked at least six miles and it was starting to get dark. The look of fear on my mum's face only added to the guilt I felt, and I just wanted to walk even more.

There would be many times whilst running, swimming, and dancing where the memories of my attempted suicide would return to me.

Why had I not succeeded?

Why had God let me live?

Why had the painkillers and vodka not killed me?

When training to be a chef and hotel manager at college, surrounded by those incredibly sharp knives, why had I looked at them and wondered why I hadn't chosen to slit my wrists instead?

Thoughtful to the end, because doing it that way would have meant mess for others to clear up after I was gone. Even in the fog of wanting to end it all, I'd always thought of those I'd leave behind, so why would I even consider suicide, one of the most selfish acts one could perform?

There was a reason I had survived, I just had to discover it, and figure out what I was born to do.

At the age of eighteen, three years after my first suicide attempt, I met my now ex-husband, the man who would become the father of my children, the man who I'd create a great deal of success with, who would challenge me beyond even my wildest imagination. I would see parts of the world I'd dreamed about, walks the lands of the prophets, eat food without guilt and I would confide in him things that had been weighing down heavy on my soul for as long as I could remember. He would become the air I needed to live, the air I needed to open my wings and soar higher than I'd ever dreamed possible. He would become the love of my life, the man I consciously chose to have children with, and the man I would build my first business with. He would become my best friend and lifelong confidant. He would also have to get used to me going for my long walks without notice.

Upon leaving college I knew I'd only really done the course because it taught me all the aspects of running a business, something I'd wanted to do for as long as I could remember. Wearing a suit jacket and pretending to call people, sharing with them my latest business ideas, writing cheques out to myself and to charities, imaginary team members and having my mum tell me I was a 'bossy little madam' - something I look back on and smile about these days.

Was this world of make believe and pretend the reason I'd not succeeded in my suicide attempt?

Were those cheques I was writing out to charities and giving to other people for the jobs they did in my business the reasons I was born to live?

Was I really destined to live an abundant life?

Not that I used the word abundant back then, I didn't really understand abundance, but I always wanted to know how people made millions and how they got to live the lifestyles I dreamed of.

I wanted to travel, I wanted to just go, have, do and learn whatever it was I wanted to without restrictions. I would imagine handing over my payment cards and walking away with whatever it was I wanted, so I started making another list. I say another list because I had always made lists of things I wanted. I had known since the age of fourteen that I would have two boys, four years apart by the age of thirty. It was written down in my diary, along with many other things I wanted.

So why had I attempted suicide at the age of fifteen if I knew I would have children and have this amazing life?

None of it made sense to me, but I kept making the lists. I kept asking the questions, and I kept dancing, swimming, running and reading.

Every now and then I'd go back through my dairies, and I was fascinated to see repetitive emotions and thoughts coming up. Noticing certain patterns emerging and the things that were making me sad, environments where I felt alone even when surrounded by others and seeing them helped me figure out which areas of my life I needed to focus on.

My parents and ex-husband wouldn't like it when I brought certain things up and would tell me to just 'leave it' whatever 'it' happened to be; but how could I when these areas of my life were not making me happy?

Re-reading my diaries I would notice all the things I'd achieved and get a great sense of achievement as I ticked everything off. I also added more wants to the list, and before I knew it my life until the age forty was all mapped out. I had many goals in life and it wouldn't be long before my business and the biggest adventure of my life, becoming a mother, soon became realities.

By the time I was nineteen my now ex-husband and I had bought our first home together, by the time I was twenty-one we were married and had our first business. By the age of twenty-four I had my second and third businesses. Things were going well career wise. I was speaking at events, leading workshops, mentoring other young women in business and coaching others.

By the time I had reached the age of twenty-five I was developing community projects, MCing at charity events and speaking at political hustings on a variety of gender, cultural diversity, and social justice issues.

I was also about to become a mother for the first time, and in true high achiever style, I wanted to have a natural birth, and being a lover of the water, I wanted a water birth. I had it all written down in my diary from start to finish. There would be no drugs, just water, gas and air (I didn't consider these to be drugs) combined with my warrior woman mentality. I was going for it, and it seemed everything I wanted, everything I wrote down was coming true, so I had no reason to doubt that I would get the birth I wanted.

Unfortunately, either I or my soon to be born son were a tad impatient and I ended up having to have the drug Diamorphine, where I lost a good twelve hours of my life on one of the most elusive trips I'd ever had; and I'd been a fan of acid on the few occasions I'd experienced it.

I still got my water birth though and nearly ended up pulling my ex-husband into the birthing pool with me. I also came close to breaking his fingers during one of the final moments of pushing out our son. Luckily, he remained dry, and all his fingers were still intact allowing him to hold our son.

I was incredibly happy, married to a bloody gorgeous man, had a beautiful home, and yet there was always a dark cloud floating around me, ready to shower me in sadness. I put it down to hormones, and we started buying vitamin B6 and B12 for me to swallow on a daily basis. My husband even joked he was going to buy me a huge bottle of both for my birthday each year.

I had chosen to not go raving anymore . How could I, when I wanted to focus on being the very best version of myself? Raving didn't fit into the image of the woman I saw myself becoming.

I swapped out the dancing for aerobics and Body Pump down at the gym, along with a spinning class. They all played hard house and trance music, giving me my music fix.

Adding these new classes into my weekly routine of rowing and swimming almost daily, plus the walking and dancing, meant I was in the best shape and level of fitness in my life.

The baby weight fell off, not there was much as I had still been exercising almost daily, including the day I went into labour.

Journalling daily, writing down everything I wanted for myself, my son and our family gave me focus. Business goals were written in a separate journal, and I was continuing a practice of planning my day into five-minute increments which I'd learnt at the age of twenty-one.

I knew what I wanted, and I was going after it, unfortunately my single focus and dogged determination was alienating me from almost everyone I knew, without me even realising it. The more I learnt, the more I succeeded the more I wanted to succeed and learn.

My parents, my mum especially was always telling me nothing was ever good enough for me, and I was making my husband feel inadequate. I was, apparently, treading on far too many of the shoes of the women in my business network and I was learning the hard way, the painful way, and some would say the only way, that life on the way to the top was lonely.

Soon after our son was born my husband started working overseas, and I was left to run the day to day of the business, the community projects and take care of all household duties. I noticed he was becoming more and more distant on his return home but put that down to the fact that I wanted to cram everything into the weekend when he was home, whilst also wanting to sleep because I was so tired from dealing with everything by myself.

It was a catch twenty-two situation because when I was awake, I just wanted to be with him, talk with him, make love with him and sort out all the much-needed tasks in the weekend that needed to be sorted out, mainly to fulfil the list of goals and targets I'd set for us.

When we were not meeting up in the family home, we would be meeting up in London at a training centre, baby son in tow and making things work. When he went back overseas, I processed everything by taking a time out by going for a long walk or going for a swim. Length after length, footstep after footstep, I'd just keep going, lost in the purging of thoughts, not stopping until the thoughts were clear, and I had a resolve to whatever it was that was going through my mind.

Sometimes my son would be so fast asleep in the pushchair by the time we got back to the house, I would leave him in the pushchair asleep whilst I crashed out on the couch. I put it down to the 'price of success'.

By the time I had reached the age of twenty-seven I had smashed all the goals I had set myself up until the age of forty. Sitting outside a friend's home, I remember crying, feeling so utterly lost and depressed I didn't know what to do. I told him I felt as though everything was falling apart. He told me to get a grip and make new list, then I would know what to do; and he was right.

As soon as I'd made that new list everything felt better. I now had a new direction, well not new, just clearer. The list of things I'd been adding to the bottom of my lists were not inspiring me, they were not big enough, they were not scary enough, they didn't excite me because I knew they would be easy to achieve.

So, I went bigger, bolder and at one point I thought I'd gone way to far that the ideas were so big 'no one like me' could achieve them. I remember sharing them with my husband at the time and he just laughed.

I felt hurt and felt as though I was aiming too high. Who was I to dream that big when he was thinking of making £200,000 a year and I was thinking of millions?

Who was I to have that much money?

Who was I to have my own seaside property, boat and multiple companies all under one parent company?

Who was I to fly first class and have a brand-new car with personalised plates?

I was a nobody. I was just a farmer's daughter from East Anglia who hadn't even got a degree to her name.

I felt myself being filled with self-doubt like I had in the past, and I noticed the feelings of depression returning. I started looking through my diaries and then I went deep into reflection and prayer. Looking back on my life I realised every time I'd taken drugs, I was dancing with death again and again, using them as a way of escaping from the pain and the loneliness I felt, even when surrounded by others.

Realising that when I had no direction, I felt lost. I also noticed that when others didn't believe in me or showed me that didn't want me around, the feelings of rejection were heightened.

Even though I'd never felt like I truly belonged anywhere but had always managed to put a smile on my face and 'play the part' everyone else needed me to play for them, which in return gave me the part I needed to learn how to play for myself.

The shy girl who did drama to come out of her shell, became a great performer on the stage of life and the one who wore make up as a mask to hide behind. The businesswoman who hid behind her business, every day a great day because God forbid anyone knew about a bad day because that would mean the business was in trouble and uncertainty spreads like a cancerous fire fuelled by the North Sea winds.

I was incredibly happy on so many levels, but the dark cloud was always ever present. I just couldn't shake it. A year went by, and I realised that if I was to fulfil my motherhood goals of having two children then my husband and I had better soon get jiggy with it again, because maybe that was what was going on?

The need to gift my first-born son the baby brother I had planned all those years ago. Not sticking to the plan had been the problem before and running out of things to do on the plan had heighten the anxiety so that must be the answer.

I shared this with my husband, and he said he was thinking it was about time for us to have our second child. There were four years between him and his brother, and so I came off the pill again ready to have another baby. Three months after coming off the pill and I was pregnant again; and I started to realise the migraines that had plagued me also stopped. I noted this down in my diary and then forgot about it.

As I journaled through my second pregnancy I started wondering if I could ever love my second child as much as I loved my first. How was it possible to love another person as much as I loved my son? I didn't even love my husband as much as I loved our son, so how could I love another child?

I also remember writing down and praying to God that I didn't want a baby who was as big as my first born and how around the same weight would be good. Little did I know that this prayer would be answered by me falling incredibly ill with HELLP Syndrome (Higher Enzymes Lower Liver Platelets) nearly killing me and my unborn child in the process with his birth coming at almost six weeks early.

Where my first-born son weighed 2.58kg, my second son weighed 2.85kg. Same numbers just in a different order and I remember thinking 'Thank God he was six weeks early!' Can you imagine if he had arrived full term how much he would have weighed! I learnt in that moment to be careful what I prayed for, and to get more precise on the various aspects of my future.

Shortly after our second son was born under life threatening conditions, both of us on life support and me with a caesarean section, my husband was called back overseas on a work contract. I would now have to heal from the birth by myself and with the love and support of some very dear friends I had made. They were not best pleased with my husband and looking back now, the depression I sank into was the realisation that our marriage was in trouble. I remember thinking as he left the house that he didn't love me enough to stay and take care of me and the boys, choosing instead to run away to the life he was building overseas. I didn't dare voice those thoughts though, especially with my track record of things I spoke and wrote coming true, so I carried on carrying on.

Once I was given the all clear to drive after the c-section, I was back at work and both my boys were coming with me to meetings.

This wasn't how I had imagined being a married mother of two boys with a business. Driving to yet another meeting I remember bursting into tears. I wanted to be a stay-at-home mum, the mummy who didn't have to work to pay for everything, the wife who was taken care of by her husband, not the wife and mother who was trying to hold it all together, pretending everything was OK.

What had gone wrong with the plan I had set in place?

Why was my husband never home to be with us?

Why did mealtimes consist of me and the boys with their dad on speakerphone?

The feelings of being ungrateful for the wonderful life we had, has resurfaced.

What did I really have to be ungrateful about?

Our eldest was now enrolled into one of the top day schools in the UK, we had successful businesses by most people's standards, we had a wonderful family home, money in the bank and we had our health.

So why was I so depressed?

Why had I got this sinking feeling that everything was going so badly wrong?

I went to the doctors and my doctor told me that these feelings I was experiencing were normal for women who had been through such a traumatic birth and early delivery; and it was especially common with mothers who had been given a c-section. I had what they called Severe Post Natal Depression and was prescribed some very strong anti-depressants. I had to take one tablet twice a day and go back and let my doctor know how I was getting on.

She was also going to send the health visitor round to check on me and the boys to make sure I was coping.

Coping? I didn't "cope". I was Dawn!

I was a successful businesswoman; I was a go-getter. I was smart, intelligent and the woman other women went to for advice on how to have it all. I didn't "cope", and yet I knew having someone check on me and the boys was probably the smartest move, and I had the feeling that the doctor knew me better than I thought she did.

Arriving home, I remember looking at myself in the mirror. I hated what I saw. I was grossly overweight, looked more tired than I had dared to even imagine was possible and I didn't not recognise the woman staring back at me. I felt ashamed of myself for letting myself go so much. How embarrassed must my husband be of me? No wonder he didn't want to stick around! And what an embarrassment I must be for my son at the school gates amongst the mums who were all so beautifully turned out in their size eight and ten designer clothes and toned bodies. Cooking the dinner that night I looked at the knife lying on the countertop. Thoughts of cutting away my ugly fat tore through my mind faster than a bolt of lightning. My boys deserved better. I had let them down. I had let my husband down and I had let my parents down.

Standing looking out the window, the tears rolled down my face. How had things gone so badly wrong? I didn't want to admit defeat by taking the anti-depressants, but I didn't want to feel like this either. I took the first pill and made a promise to myself I would get in shape. I would look for a competition and enter it as soon as the boys went to bed.

When my husband called that night for the family mealtime, he was yet again distracted by work. I told him I had been to the doctors, and she had prescribed anti-depressants, and that I had made a promise to myself to get in shape. He told me whatever I wanted to do he would support me. For the first time in our marriage, I didn't believe him, so I tested him and told him I was going to take up pole dancing, and he chuckled and said, "Well if that's what you want to do, I am not going to stop you". I thought he hadn't been listening, but he had, and I felt even worse for doubting him. What the hell was going on inside my head?

A few weeks later I told him I thought we needed to see a marriage counsellor, he hesitated and then he agreed. When the appointment finally came around, I sat crying my eyes out and the only words I remember to this day are "If you are not careful and do not start to take more notice of her, she is not going to be around much longer, and I don't mean by divorce either." He looked at me, sadness in his eyes, and yet the distance between us was so obvious. I was blaming him for leaving me to deal with everything, and he was drowning in his own thoughts, whatever they were.

Once I had started on the anti-depressants I began to sleep better, and yet one day whilst driving home after picking up my eldest son from school, with my youngest crying in his seat, I remember this awful feeling of just wanting to end it all. I looked down at the speedometer, looked up to see how far ahead the car in front was, and tried to work out how fast I needed to drive to kill myself and yet keep the boys from being hurt. Tears burnt the back of my eyes. What kind of mother leaves her children by crashing the car? What did I have to feel sad about? As soon as we were home, I took another anti-depressant. I couldn't have any more thoughts like that, I just couldn't; and yet I did. Not just once, but many times. I thought about taking all the anti-depressants in one go like I had my mum's tablets back when I was fifteen, but my husband had to be home to deal with the boys. I couldn't leave them without care and supervision. I thought about driving the car into a wall, into the river, I even looked up how to attach a hose to the exhaust and gas myself. I even tried to figure out how long it would take for our open plan home to fill with gas before I lit a candle, and the house went BOOM! Not once though did I think of cutting my wrists though.

One day I received a letter from the doctor informing me of another appointment to see her to 'see how I was getting on'. She increased the dosage of the anti-depressants to 250mg and within a day I started to feel so much better; but it wasn't real. It wasn't me. It was the drugs that made me feel better, and if I had come off narcotics before because I wanted to achieve the same high, they gave me, you can bet your arse I was going to do the same with these anti-depressants!

So, I started journaling again, going even deeper than I had before. I looked at where I had stopped, and I looked at my list of achievements, and my current list of goals. I hadn't journaled for months; in fact, it was almost a year since I had journaled. No wonder I felt the way I did. Writing had always been my outlet, my sanity check. Making lists of things I wanted to experience, all the things I wanted to achieve, places I had wanted to go and the kind of wife and mother I wanted to be, these lists were my safety nets. So, I set to work, I started writing as if my life depended on it, because it did!

I wrote list after list after list, getting really clear on the kind of woman I wanted to be too, the kind of example I wanted to set my boys about what it was to be human, and live a full and exciting life. As my lists got longer, and I went through journal after journal, I tore the pages of doubts, fears and overwhelm placing them in the fire pit with a prayer. Immediately I started to feel better. I was alchemising everything I wanted into existence and turning the negative emotions into courage, confidence and excitement.

A few months later I told my husband, I want to stop taking the tablets and make the move to Egypt, like we planned, and if we don't do it then, it would be too late. I didn't know what it would be too late for, but he said "OK, when do you want to come off the tablets?" I told him I hadn't taken the tablets at all for the last three days because having done my research it was going to be between days three and five that the cold turkey would kick in. He looked shocked, but not surprised. I had done my research and he knew I had timed it for his return home.

With the boys in bed that night I lay on the couch waiting for my husband to come down. I was already starting to feel twitchy and nauseous and knew the cold turkey process was starting. I started to get really hot and yet cold at the same time, and as the evening progressed, I started vomiting and convulsing. It wasn't a seizure by any means but as I relaxed into it all and allowed the process of healing to take over, I remembered telling myself I had to have this poison out of my body by the end of the weekend as he was leaving again on the first Monday morning flight.

I stayed in bed all that weekend, the boys enjoying movie time with their dad whilst I rested upstairs. They made me pancakes and cups of tea to make me feel better, and sure enough by the end of Sunday night, I did feel better. The next ten days I put myself on a cleansing detox removing things such as sugar, dairy, wheat, yeast, processed foods out of my diet. Alcohol was not something I drank so that didn't need to be removed, and there was no way I was giving up tea, so caffeine remained.

I then started putting the plans in place for us all to move to Egypt. I had the plan, I worked the plan, and the plan got bigger, and bigger with everything starting to fall into place again. I was happier, and I knew I had found the solution for me, and today the solutions of dancing, walking, swimming, reading and journalling are my 'sanity savers'.

Now as I look back on my life over the last twelve years, the list of things I wrote down, have all come true. I may now be divorced, but I am happier by myself. The business I have now by myself is more successful than any business I have ever had. I no longer hate the skin I'm in, in fact I love my body. I have fallen madly truly in love with the woman I am today. I've been through hell and back enough times to deserve the love I give myself, because I never allowed myself to quit.

I have my two children to thank for me being alive today because if it weren't for them, I know I would have gone through with ending it all back in the early days after my Post Natal Depression. I reached out, I got help and I made a plan.

I now sail around the world leading and inspiring other women to live their dreams, coaching clients into how to create a vision for their life, sharing their stories and publishing their own books, so others like me who needed to look for the answers in books can find them. Those who need to know they're not alone, and that there are people out there who get it, can find the hope and courage to just keep putting one foot in front of the other. Books hold the answers to so many things in the world, from escapism to courage, for us to discover more about ourselves and the world we live in, to facing the demons lurking in the shadows of our minds.

When people reach out to me filled with gratitude, having read something I've written, sharing with me the impact my words have had on them, I'm so grateful to them. I am grateful that I never succeeded in my attempted suicides, and that I never died all those times I took drugs or followed through on the dark thoughts in my head.

Had I succeeded, I would never have been able to serve so many people around the world, and I would not have been able to witness my two incredible sons grow up into the fine young men they are today.

I have been able to fulfil my dream of being paid to read and write books for a living, speaking on stages and travelling the world. I've been able to have the opportunity to pay people to work for me, gifting them the opportunity to provide for their families, allowing them to live their dream lives.

The woman I dreamed of being, the one with money who dreamed of doing great things with it, I get to do these days. I get to be that 'Bossy Little Madam' my mother used to call me, and I get to provide a great life for my sons, leading my children to greatness, encouraging them, my nieces and others to follow their dreams.

I am living the dream. I am filled with love and gratitude each and every day. The dark clouds have gone as have the migraines which never returned because I never went back on the pill.

My days are always filled with sunshine because each day I get to start afresh, living in a state of gratitude for every breath I take. I'm grateful my mum named me Dawn, because with each new sunrise I get to give life another go, for me, my boys, and for all of you reading this book.

Thank you for choosing this book, for showing up for yourself and those in your life. Remember, you get to be who you choose to be, all you have to do is make the right choices.

Choose life, choose you and choose gratitude, always.

With love,

Dawn x

REFLECTIONS

REFLECTIONS

REFLECTIONS

Cheryl Blunt

Entrepreneur/Philanthropist/Personal Development & Business Coach/Speaker
Owner/Operator of Kids Retreat, LLC
Founder of Kids Retreat Family Corporation Non-profit
Cheryl Blunt Enterprises, LLC – I Came Out of It

"I CAME OUT OF IT" From VICTIM to being VICTORIOUS through all the challenges that life presented me. After years of suffering in silence, sexual abuse, domestic violence, prostitution, suicide attempts, and multiple addictions, I was finally set free and given another opportunity to live life on my own terms. My goal and mission are to be a positive role model, coach, and speaker in helping guide women, children, and families with learning and growing through their challenges while assisting them in navigating and creating a healthier living environment.

For more information about how to support or get involved with our non-profit. Go to **www.kidsretreatfamily.org** or follow us on Facebook @kidsretreatfamilynonprofit or @kidsretreat, LLC. If you would like help, guidance, and support in how to give back to your community, contact me for a free information pack by emailing cblunt@kidsretreatfamily.org or using our email portal at **https://kidsretreatfamily.org**

Out of It

BY CHERYL BLUNT
USA

It was a tough time for me growing up. The things I had to go through; a child should never have to go through on their own.

One week after I was born my grandmother passed away. My mother lost her mother right after she brought me home from the hospital. This is significant because this was supposed to be the beginning of the bonding process with my mother that never happened between us. As a child, my mother always seemed disconnected which left me with no connection to her. From the first moment of my memories, I was always searching to be loved, wanted, cared for, and protected.

When I was eleven years old my parents divorced. As like with most children who experience the divorce of their parents, it was very emotional and traumatic for me. It was also an extremely critical time in my life, the time when I was going through puberty and transitioning into a young lady or at least that was the plan. My parents were trying to adjust to being single and dealing with their own identity crisis during this time. Little did I know that things were drastically about to change for my brothers and I too. I loved my father. I was a true daddy's girl. It broke my heart to not be able to be with my father, and only seeing him for a few hours at a time and sometimes not at all. During this adjustment period my mother began to work a lot and my brothers, and I were beginning to learn how to take care of ourselves.

It was during this period, at age eleven that a friend of the family molested me. He knocked on the door after my mother had gone out for the evening. He said he was coming over to check on us and I let him in, unaware that he couldn't be trusted. My brothers were in the other room playing. I was scared and I didn't know what to do or how to fight him off. I sat on the couch and cried after he left. That was the day that changed everything for me. I was ashamed, I was angry, I was scared, I was hurt, I was devastated and blamed myself for opening the door. My brothers were there, what was I thinking? How could I have not protected us better.

After this incident, I started becoming very distant, quick to get angry, destructive, having problems in school, and sometimes not attending school at all. I hated myself and felt like everybody else hated me too. I did not understand and could not process what had happened. I was on my own with not much parental support. I didn't know how to express myself, and I was scared to tell anyone. I was ashamed of myself, I felt dirty, and I did not know where to turn for help.

When you are physically and mentally abused by people who are supposed to love you, you tend to blame yourself for everything. I learned at a very young age to keep secrets and hide my feelings. I found if I told the truth or even mentioned anything I was feeling, it would set off a chain reaction in people that I was not quite mature or old enough to deal with. There were several instances where I would leave and not come home for hours and sometimes days. I would hang out in the streets with some of my older friends. I felt safe with them, they were like mothers to me. They became my family. There were many times when my mother would be looking for me and I would be places where I shouldn't be. I wanted to be anywhere but at home.

Not too long after I turned twelve years old, my mother thought it was best for me to go live with my father. I'm not sure that was the best decision for me since my father worked several jobs. The transition to my father's house would mean that I would pretty much be on my own again.

I started hanging out in the streets more and rarely going to school. I began drinking, smoking, and using several different kinds of drugs. I absolutely had no respect for myself or anyone else. I was embarrassed because I never knew how to be a young lady. I seemed to be always carrying the burdens of an adult, not a little girl.

At the age of fourteen, I found myself in the hands of a convicted criminal who had just gotten out of prison two weeks prior. I was abducted, brutally raped and sodomized at gunpoint. I was taken to an apartment where I could hear children upstairs, and the adults in the home chose to ignore my screams, my cries, and what was happening to me. It made me sick to know that they had children, and they would let a child be sexually abused in their presence. I thought to myself nobody really cares about me, so why should I? Early the next morning, I could hear the kids upstairs getting ready for school. He rushed me out of that apartment to another abandoned apartment nearby. I ended up in this apartment begging for my life. He would ponder and hold the gun to my head and pull it away, several times. I was terrified because I knew what he was capable of. With a lot of begging, pleading, and promises, he let me go. That morning I had to walk about two to three miles or more to get back home. I was dishevelled, I was distraught, my clothes were torn, I was dirty, my hair was all over my head. I kept wondering what I did to deserve this life. It felt like the long walk of shame.

When I reached my home, I did not want to go in. I did not want to give another lame excuse about why I did not come home that night. I had been trying so hard that week to do what was right. I was hurting, I had bruises, I was scared, and I was in tears. I was not sure what to do or who to call, so I decided to make that call to suicide because I thought nobody cared. That was it for me. That was my first attempt at suicide.

I sat on my father's porch and tried to cut myself several times on the wrist. That didn't work, so I went inside to find some pills. I took all the ones I could find. I slept for hours. I do not even remember what day it was when I woke up, I woke up sick and dazed. I was hoping that I did not wake up at all. At that very moment, I thought I'd died, even though

I was not dead. I was wishing that the man who'd raped me and held a gun to my head had just killed me right then and there. There was no other reason for me to live at that point.

After that happened, I lost my heart, my will to live, love or care. I began a journey on a downward spiral of self-hate. I started using drugs more heavily and drinking more to numb the pain. I started hanging out with a completely different crowd and was recruited into sex trafficking and prostitution. I began selling my body for money, drugs, and because I thought that was all I had to offer anybody. You name it, I tried it. I was prostituting myself for anything I needed. I did whatever I had to do to survive, and everyone in my hometown knew my name and how it identified me.

I am only sharing this dark part of my life because I want you to know what set the rest of my life in motion. With all these things happening in my life, it was easy to give up, it was easy to believe I had nothing to live for. I decided at that point that I did not care anymore, and I was going to be just who they thought I was nothing.

There was so much that I kept silent about and so much that was going on with me that I did not tell my family or close friends. I continued to live a life of destruction, hurting anyone that got in the way and destroying myself at the same time. The anger and betrayal that I felt had grown so large inside of me, that I would try several times to end my life or try to make someone end it for me. My family was now in the streets. The older women of my hometown were like my mentors. They taught me and guided me through a lot of challenging times in my life. At this time, I felt as though I was the black sheep of my family. They did not expect any good from me at that point in my life and I did not give any good back.

At age seventeen, I moved to Dallas Texas, with my thirty-one-year-old boyfriend. We lived in hotels for months on end. I was there alone without any family. I stopped doing drugs when I became pregnant, but I continued my bad behaviour, and I had our daughter in August of 1985. I tried to settle down for a minute and then I finally left the volatile and abusive relationship that it was.

My daughter and I ended up at the domestic violence shelter in Indianapolis Indiana. Where I went through extensive counselling and therapy. They put us in a Public Housing Unit called Brick City, and I had now stopped doing all drugs. I settled into a routine of catching the bus from the southside of Indianapolis to the north side, dropping off my baby at day-care, and catching the bus again downtown to a place for employee development training. I started taking classes the State was offering to those who signed up for state benefits. The training was called Training, Inc. This is significant because I was in the last phase of training in 1986 - 1987 when there was a knock on the door of my apartment. It was my ex, my daughter's father. He had just picked up some cocaine and it was an extremely large amount. I knew that this was a trigger for me, and I knew that I couldn't be around it, but I chose to let him come in and stay for a while, knowing that I could lose my place and lose my life all at the same time.

During this time, which was a span of approximately a month, I was barely going to school. We smoked crack cocaine all day long. My daughter looked a complete mess. My house was a mess. We were cooking crack and smoking all day and night. One day I woke up sick, throwing up and that is something that I never do. I went to the clinic after I left class that day and they told me I was pregnant. I was so devastated. I could not believe that I was finally trying to get my life together and I was pregnant and using drugs again, a complete re-lapse. I went back home and told him to get out. He left and that night I cried. I was looking for some cocaine to get high and I was literally on my knees looking for anything that may have dropped on the floor. My baby was watching me, she was hungry, and she had this look on her face like "Mummy what is wrong?" I looked at her and I had not done her hair in days, and she had the same filthy clothes on. She was dirty and I looked at myself; I was filthy and dirty. At that point, I called my parents to see if one of them could come and get my daughter for a while. I took her to my parents, came home, and again I was on my knees searching for any piece of cocaine that I could find to smoke. I ended up in the corner with my coat still on, sweating profusely and crying because I was in pain. I started bleeding and coughing but I knew I had to go to class the next morning. I called the school and told them that I couldn't make it. Very clearly, I heard my counsellor in the background state that if I was not in attendance that day then I would be cut from classes. Mind you, I had never finished anything, I never cared about anything. I still hated myself and what had happened to me.

But that day was different.

I did not want to be labelled a quitter any longer, I did not want to give up on myself anymore. I wanted to finish. I got up, got myself together as much as I could, and rode the bus to class. I remember being sick as a dog in and out of the bathroom throwing up at school. I was not only going through drug detox, but I was also losing my baby. To make a long story short I went through months of detox alone in my apartment throwing up sweating and going to class every morning. I did it at home without medication which others do in detox at a hospital. I completed it alone. I was a mess, but I did graduate from the program, and I got a job, a really good job in downtown Indianapolis.

I continued to run from my past. I ended up moving to California in 1988, where I met my soon-to-be husband. I was still reeling from the drugs, still hadn't healed from my past, so I continued making bad decisions. I started using new drugs: Meth was now my drug of choice. That was my coping mechanism at the time. I was transitioning into a new life in a new place, and I was not sure how to stay clean, something was missing. I was still using, not being financially responsible, nor taking care of myself the way I should have been. I didn't really start getting my life back on track until 1990, when we started discussing marriage. I stopped using everything but alcohol. It was a tough road, but I was able to completely leave drugs behind.

On the 19th of April 1991, I got married. We had moved from California to Virginia, to be closer to my husband's family. It was during our marriage that I realised that I had not completely healed. I was very insecure, and I tried to hold on with all my might. At the time, I felt like that was all the family I really had. I never quite knew how to be a part of a family unit. I felt inadequate and lost, and I still had random thoughts of suicide from time to time. During our marriage, I fell ill to Cushing's Syndrome. They started treating me with several different drugs. I already had an addictive personality so these drugs triggered a severe reaction in me.

I found my breaking point around 2006 when I had a nervous breakdown. I was in and out of the mental health and drug ward for several years. I had become extremely ill. They had me on several different medications. I was taking three different kinds of painkillers, in fact everything and anything they could think of to give me. I had totally reached my peak of self-destruction. I hated myself and I was a detriment to anyone and everyone around me. I tried to take my life several times during that period. I needed help and I did not know where to turn.

During my last stay in the hospital between 2007-2008. All the trauma from my childhood came flooding in and I sat there with tears rolling down my face, wondering how I had gotten to this point. I was drowning in hopelessness, clinical depression, suicidal thoughts, anger, anxiety, and some deep-rooted pain.

At that moment, I had a choice to make. Either I was going to try one more time to take my life and leave all this pain behind, or I was going to live this life that I had been so blessed with and live it to the fullest.

I was at a crossroads. I felt like I was drowning, and I was at the lowest point of my life. I was not sure if I had the stamina to fight back anymore. I was totally helpless to take care of my children, my family and completely helpless to take care of myself. I had all but given in.

One day my daughter came to see me as I was sitting behind the bars at the hospital. I was loaded on medication and did not know if I was coming or going. I could see my daughter's face as she was walking into the hospital. I could see the hurt and brokenness on her face. She said, "Mummy, I am worried, I don't think you are going to make it out of here this time." She was twenty-two years old. I looked at her with a blank look on my face, I did not tell her then, but I did not think I was going to make it out either or if I would ever see my beautiful children again. Tears just started rolling down my face, I had no answers for her. She told me I had to fight to come home. We sat there in silence for a moment, neither one of us knowing what to say and how this would turn out. I felt like a total failure.

After a few days in the hospital and thinking about my precious children who did not deserve all I had taken them through, I decided to start taking my therapy seriously and make the adjustments needed to become well again.

After a few years of trying to recover I landed a job in 2010, with a contractor working with the State of Indiana. I started getting back on my feet. At that time, I was on Social Security, and I was told by my doctors and everyone else that I could no longer work *and* that I would never work again. I was still struggling internally during this period and my marriage was slowly dissolving. My children were suffering the most. I was not present, in the moment and their father worked a lot and was also not present. We were a functioning dysfunctional family.

In 2012 I left my husband. I decided that I'd had enough of the infidelity, fighting, arguing, and emotional abuse that we were causing each other. I was ready to take my life back and give my children the life that they so deserved and move us to a new level of living. I was ready to face all my fears and fight to get my life on track. I no longer wanted to be a victim of my past; I wanted to be victorious in my future.

MY TRANSITION

I started making changes to adjust to life on my own with my children. My two oldest children were over eighteen and living out of the home. I just had my baby boy who was fourteen years old at the time. I was heartbroken about my marriage, and I had never wanted my children to be without their father. I will not even pretend to make you think that this transition was easy, because it was far from it. It was very difficult for me and my children.

I had several setbacks and I fell into old ways of thinking, and the relationships and friendships that I used to have in the past. I started searching for love again because after all, I only knew my worth in sex and relationships. I began hanging out at the bars, hanging out with people that I should not have been with, looking up old relationships, and dating again. It just felt good to be free again. All I wanted to do was go back to what I knew. I still was not aware of my worth at that point.

Once I recognized the trap I was falling into, I started to heal deep within, I had to leave the crowd. I had to walk away from things that were not good for me and walk alone to get to where I needed to be. I had beaten the addictions: I had moved past the crowd. This was no time for me to start going in reverse. Going backward was not an option for me. I had to turn around and move forward.

This was a time to be brave and move towards a new and brighter future. Being brave is not going backward but moving away from the old and into a new way of life. My new journey was going to change my life and it was going to catapult me and my children into a new level of living. So, I started taking inventory of what I needed to do right now to get back on track for good. I wanted to start living up to my true potential.

My first goal was to heal from within and learn what made me who I am. What did I like? What did I need? I started deep holistic therapy. My goal was to answer the constant stream of questions in my head. The therapy revealed things about myself that I never knew. It allowed me to explore my bottled-up feelings and emotions that I had kept hidden and silent for so long. This intense therapy helped me identify my needs, my wants, and what I was made of.

I had to start identifying my triggers and avoid them, as well as have a plan in place, with coping mechanisms in place for when they occurred. Understanding what my triggers were so I could avoid setbacks and relapses. This was huge for me because I did not want to go backward in my walk forward. I started identifying what made me suicidal, what my mindset and thought processes were, and most of all, how could I improve myself. These are some of the important questions that you need to ask yourself when you are transitioning to another level in life.

First, look at some of the early signs that you may need to seek help:
- ✓ You are feeling sad and depressed
- ✓ Feeling empty, hopeless, trapped, or having no reason to live
- ✓ Extremely sad, anxious, or agitated
- ✓ Unbearable emotional or physical pain
- ✓ Extreme mood swings
- ✓ Using drugs or alcohol more
- ✓ Eating or sleeping more or less
- ✓ Withdrawing

I began mending and building relationships with both my parents. My mother and I had been estranged for several years during my teenage years and early twenties. We stayed in touch and my mother helped me by taking care of my kids during my stay in the hospital, but we had not cleared the air by discussing our emotions or how broken our relationship was. We started communicating and spending more time together. I started reaching out to my father more, and I took a trip to spend some one-on-one time with him. I started spending more time with my brothers as well. Our family had been totally separated from each other and we were all living in separate states. We had all been emotionally disconnected for a long time and I was ready to break down the walls that were keeping us apart.

I ran for years. I ran from myself and the reputation that I had created. I only knew one way to live and that was in the struggle, in the dirt, and in the mud. I did not know any other way. Statistically, I should not have made it. Coming from a broken home, drug addict, suicidal, alcoholic, raped, molested, prostitute, sex trafficked, domestic violence, homelessness, I really should not be here to tell this story. All I knew was that now my only focus was to soar like the eagle I was meant to be. I did not want to be shackled any longer, I did not want to be held back, I did not want to live under anyone else's set of rules. I wanted to be free to think, to act, and to make my own decisions as to what was best for me. I wanted to fly high like my spirit was meant to soar. The years of domination under other people had taken a toll on me. It was time to learn who I was and what I liked.

My journey to get back on my feet consisted of:
- ✓ Daily prayer and meditation
- ✓ Making a self-care routine
- ✓ Asking for help when I needed it
- ✓ Journaling - I had always journaled, but I decided to go a step further and journal my entire recovery experience. I journaled how I was feeling each day, questions I was asking, new things that I had learned, and what I would experience after praying and meditation. I used journaling as a tool to get through the craziness. It was very calming for me, and I could go back and measure my progress.
- ✓ Taking one moment at a time
- ✓ Facing my fears
- ✓ Setting Boundaries
- ✓ Losing my toxic traits and negative thinking
- ✓ Setting defined goals
- ✓ No more procrastinating
- ✓ And knowing "I am important"

Now

In 2017 my divorce was final, and I found out my son was sick with Crohn's Disease. I decided that I was going to put my all into turning my life and family around. My kids deserved so much better from me and life.

I left everything that was not good for me behind me in 2017. The old me was finally gone. I could finally say that I had changed. From the point of my new being, I vowed to leave nothing on the table when it came to my life and my businesses. To always go hard for my goals and to always operate out of love, courage, and truth.

I quit my job as a Customer Service Supervisor in 2018, I had no idea that I was going to leave. I loved helping people and it was a job that I loved, and I had finally made a career for myself. I was proud I'd stayed in the job for so long. One day the unhealthy environment of the job had made me so sick, my blood pressure was up, my stomach was hurting, I could not function, and I started taking my things to my car. I was not sure what it all meant at the time, but I could not endure that kind of strain on my body and my mind any longer. The weight and the stress of what I was enduring was too much for me. I was determined if the suicide attempts, drugs, and everything else had not taken me out, this job was not going to take me out either.

I had $246.00 to my name, and I walked out never to return. I went on to start Kids Retreat that following week, a family childcare home for children under six. One month later we got the news that my daughter had a brain tumour and would have to have major surgery. I thought If we can make it through this, we can make it through anything.

I learned that it takes great courage to take steps to turn your life around, and it's ok to take small steps. Whatever I could allow myself, I did, and I always moved forward. Life is too precious to destroy, we are made for greatness.

In August 2019, I was asked to give a testimony about my past. It was in my hometown where I grew up, the same town I had left and avoided for years. I wanted to deny this request to go back and share anything at all. This is something I had always avoided. I would ride through, stop to see a few people, and hurry back out but this time was different, I knew I had to go back and help someone else. On the day of my testimony October 26, 2019, one year and a day to the moment my daughter had brain surgery, I rode through the town. It made me sad, sad to see where I used to stand in front of the liquor store, buying alcohol at fourteen and fifteen years old when I should have been in school. To see the hotels where I used to prostitute myself and where I used to live out of while doing drugs. The bar where I stayed for two weeks with an older man, and no one seemed to care. The house where I was ganged raped and sent on my way when they were all finished with me. The home I used to live in which brought back so many bad memories. The street corners where we would hang out. The back alley's where I would meet the older men in the city for favours. I began to cry, tears rolled down my face as I rode through town. This would be the beginning of a new start for me.

In December of 2019, my children, who were now fully grown, decided we would team up and combine all our experiences, and knowledge, to give back to our community. In 2014, we had started a new family tradition we called 'Our Family Outreach' and it was time to take it to another level. We created Kids Retreat Family Corporation, a non-profit organisation where we gave food, clothing, childcare, books, and resources to those in need. We were approved for our tax exemption status of 501c3 in May 2020, right during the pandemic. Having this has allowed Kids Retreat to serve more kids, women, and families in our community, and has helped us give support to other non-profit and community projects.

I have learned more in the last nine years than at any other time in my life. I have learned how to love myself, my children, and others unconditionally. I now have the chance to live out the purpose that was planned for my life. I celebrate my life now. I feel the wholeness of who I am. I know that I am enough without anyone else's opinion of me. I take chances, I take risks. I let life flow and I ride the wave. I take the experiences that I have been through, and I use them to mentor, inspire, and empower others.

It takes hard work and resilience to change. Recovery of anything is not easy, you must keep reminding yourself of the 'Why?' and the 'Who?'. Why are you doing what you are doing? Who is it you are serving? For years, I played small to make others feel better, not anymore. Now I humbly apply everything I know to serve my community and help others to do the same in their community. I used to walk around in shame, with my head down so no one would see me, now I hold my head up high because I know who I am now. I try my best to add value whenever I step into the room.

> **Here are some things I would like to share with you from my story:**
> 1. No matter how far you go in the wrong direction, it is always ok to stop and turn around.
> 2. Sometimes you must try to solve a problem more than once to win it.
> 3. Take it one day at a time, one moment at a time, one second at a time
> 4. Baby steps count as steps forward
> 5. Do not let your current situation dictate your future. You were made to thrive.
> 6. It is ok to let go of the things that no longer serve you
> 7. Do not delay, take steps now to make changes

I do the things that scare me now, I take the challenges and I do not stop until I conquer it, even if I must start over several times. Life is much more enjoyable now. I would like to challenge you to do the same. There is nothing that you cannot do. Take the steps to fight to take your life back. Ask for help if you need it, reach out to someone who can help you or seek resources. Your life is too precious to end.

I now take full responsibility for my life. I no longer blame my parents or the other adults that could have intervened. This is my life's journey, and I am now following the plan that was laid in front of me. There is no looking back, only ahead into the future.

My life, my past, I acknowledge it, I own it, and take full responsibility for it. Now I embrace everything that has been gifted to me. I used to want to change my life, but now, I would not change it for the world. It made me who I am today, and what I have become. I want people to know that I did not do this on my own. There is my creator (My Heavenly Father) and really good people who helped me along the way. I want you to know that if I came out of it, that you can too.

Yours in strength and courage,

Cheryl Blunt

For more information about how to support or get involved with our non-profit. Go to **www.kidsretreatfamily.org** or follow us on Facebook @kidsretreatfamilynonprofit or @kidsretreat, LLC

If you would like help, guidance, and support in how to give back to your community, contact me for a free information pack by emailing **cblunt@kidsretreatfamily.org**

REFLECTIONS

REFLECTIONS

Kim Levings

Kim Levings, a South Africa expat now living in Colorado, USA is an experienced and well regarded professional in the training development and coaching fields, with more than thirty-five years' experience in the field.

Following her own recovery of two suicide attempts and years of depression, Kim's passion is to unleash others from the prison of their minds. Her training and coaching systems help people in all walks of life to rethink themselves from the "inside-out" as they re-map the thinking, habits, and behaviours that drive outcomes in their lives.

A seasoned trainer, speaker, author and coach, Kim has a humorous, candid, and transparent way of communicating, which helps her make connection with people, who quickly come to like and trust her. Learn more at:

https://kimlevings.com

ReThink YOU - To Live the Life You are Created to Live

BY KIM LEVINGS
USA

**My journey from hopelessness and despair to
a life of joy and personal fulfilment**

It has been said that the attempt to take one's life is choosing a permanent solution to a temporary problem. The reality is that when you're about to do something like that, you are not thinking with a clear mind. It is not possible at that moment to view the world with a different perspective. If it were, you would not be contemplating what you are. If you have experienced those thoughts or are still stuck in them, I hope that you will find some help and guidance to get out of that hole, by reading my story.

The pain of emotional wounds is one that drives a stake into your very soul. It is a pain that can only be understood by a person who has lived with an internal wound. It's a gnawing at your internal sense of self. It's a sense of hopelessness that lives forever in the shadows of your mind, ready to be triggered when the right buttons are pushed, or when presented with a particular set of circumstances and emotional state. Left unchecked, it will slowly creep back onto the centre stage of your conscious thoughts and feelings. It will take over your internal narrative, and even turn up the volume. It will introduce lies, incorrect perspectives that inevitably result from frequent and emotionally-charged memory recall, and then it will do what it does best – replaying the soundtrack of all previous hurts. Soon, reason starts to slowly step back into the wings of your mind and the emotions are now in charge and control the centre stage.

This sounds dramatic. It is. For anyone who is currently trapped in this pattern and watching helplessly as what you *don't* want continues to come about in your life, it's a daily battle that hijacks your life. You can temporarily take back control by treating the symptoms. Correction, not treating, assuaging the symptoms. You find temporary fixes that help you shut out the drama on your stage. Drugs, whether legal and prescribed, or not, alcohol, and any form of behaviour that temporarily removes the need to deal with the actors on centre stage is the only solution that seems to present itself. Compulsive and addictive patterns are almost always the result of an unhealed emotional wound. Our attention is constantly on finding ways to alleviate the anxiety and internal symptoms that we don't like.

Not in any way do I want to undermine the impact of physical wounds and that includes trauma, sexual and other physical abuse, PTSD from major life trauma, and that suffered by many of our veterans who put their lives in the line of fire to defend our free world. I have had no physical or other abuse, nor traumatic events in my life. This is *my* story. So, I choose to speak about emotional woundedness, while understanding that many are dealing with both physical and emotional challenges.

Unresolved emotional wounds were what dragged me into a deeper and deeper depression when I was in my late teens into my twenties. The emotional wounds were not from anything major by today's world culture. I had reacted with deep grief and disappointment when my parents' marriage fell apart after being together for twenty-five years. I was only eighteen. I'd grown up in a stable, happy, loving, and generally balanced family home. I enjoyed school, friends, sports, Girl Guides, and loved the fact that we were Boxer dog breeders. Many a day was spent at dog shows or watching the adorable Boxer puppies being born.

I was the youngest of three girls and despite the inevitable fights between us, when there was always one of the three who was ostracised for some silly reason, we got along well and to this day remain remarkably close. We no doubt fought over whose turn it was to do a particularly nasty chore, and at other times we would laugh together hysterically over something quite trivial (which we still do even in our later years.) Life was good.

Then, almost imperceptibly at first, things started to change. It was when I was about thirteen, when my eldest sister had started secretarial school and my middle sister was nearing the end of high school, just as I entered that highly desired stage of life, things shifted. I can see all this now with a clarity that only comes from a place of healing and the wisdom of maturity. I can also reflect on things with a deeper understanding as a result of the work I've done on myself and with others, as a coach.

Depending on which of the three sisters you speak to, you may hear three different narratives surrounding the years of change, during which there was a slow, but steady deterioration in the fabric of our family. In a conversation with my sisters a few years back, I asked them if either of them had any pictures or vivid memories from that specific five-year period of our lives. "Huh," replied the eldest, "now that you mention it, that is strange. I haven't seen any pictures since we stopped going to Margate." We'd gone to Margate - a seaside town on the southern Kwazulu Natal coastline in South Africa - every Christmas for the entire period of our childhood. Our last trip was when I was about eleven or twelve.

The way I remember it is that it began with the changing landscape of dad's job, combined with the aging and deteriorating health of our grandparents. Dad's mother died when I was around fifteen, and he was devastated as he had never known his father. My mother's father was diagnosed with emphysema, and her mother developed heart problems. Mum suffered from depression, and it got worse. Even though she always worked part time, and maybe full time (I can't remember) there were times when she was just not herself. I noticed a growing discontent within her and found her complaining at times about dad's job, and his lack of understanding of things going on. The longer hours he spent at work, the more they seemed to drift apart.

There were also challenges between mum and dad around my middle sister, who had turned quite rebellious, and then married when she was barely eighteen to go sailing overseas with her boyfriend. Mum was far more understanding than dad and the wedge between them grew.

When you are a teenager and your parents have problems, you feel helpless and confused. Too young to speak any wisdom to them, but also old enough to recognise that things were indeed starting to come apart. I didn't understand mum's depression. To be honest, there were times when I was perhaps less than understanding and instead, felt resentful and hurt when mum was often absent from my life emotionally.

I was comparatively enamoured with the world of dad's work and soon started working Saturdays and school holidays at the wholesale store he managed. This caused the two of us to grow even closer, and I still have fond memories of driving us home from work when I had my learner's permit, and subsequently got my license. My first car also came from dad's employer, as I purchased a salesperson's VW Beetle when she was being upgraded. During those years, the distance widened between me and mum and in some ways my sisters, too. Years later, this division became so apparent and caused a lot of strife. Praise God these wounds were later healed, and we now have an incredible bond as sisters, especially as we also lost both mum and dad in the past few years.

The breakdown started happening during my first (and only) year of university. Mum had become more and more depressed and suffered from anxiety, mood swings, and other issues. I felt sorry for her but was not sure how to help.

Dad continued to work long hours, my sisters were both living overseas at that point, and mum remained distant, and self-absorbed as she struggled with her depression. I failed university, having spent more time drowning my sorrows and living a wild social life with my then boyfriend. My father was angry and told me I had two weeks to find a job, as I was no longer permitted to live there rent-free. In hindsight, it was the best thing he could have done, as my career and professional development has been the mainstay of my life ever since. I found a job at a local bank and enrolled in secretarial college in the evenings.

I broke up with my boyfriend and soon met someone new. The older brother of a colleague at the bank. He was Afrikaans and worked on the oil rigs, which meant he was gone for weeks at a time. I would count the days till he came back. During one of these "missing him" periods, one day, mum told me she was moving out because she needed a break and to be on her own to deal with her problems. Dad was enraged but I know that at the root of his anger was a deep hurt that he didn't know how else to verbalize. He had never been a nasty or aggressive person, even when angry. I remember driving to my boyfriend's parents, sobbing uncontrollably. I was in such a state of anxiety and complete breakdown, that his mother insisted I spend the night, which I did. I took off from work to recover the next day and can remember that it was the first time I'd ever had what my daughter and I now call an "ugly" cry, racking, gut-wrenching, and uncontrollable, leaving you empty.

Somehow, I put myself back together enough to drive back home. I don't remember what dad had done while I was gone. I assumed he had no doubt drank himself to sleep. I knew he was also devastated. I stepped in to take over where mum left off. Planning meals, shopping for groceries, opening the mail, supervising our then maid, etc. I become the intermediary between my parents. I was continuing at college three nights a week, too, which meant driving all the way to the city after work, attending class, and then trying to make it over to mum when I could. She lived quite a distance from us, in a furnished flat close to the city. If I didn't go and visit mum enough, she would complain and say how hurt she was. Dad continued to be frustrated and would make abrasive remarks about any topic that related to mum. I can still remember the day I had to tell her he'd closed the credit account at the pharmacy. She was angry, hurt, and said how disappointed she was. It was horrible. At nineteen, nobody wants to be the sole caretaker of parents who could not figure out how to save their marriage.

Several months later, my eldest sister returned from New Zealand, and I can remember us "pretending" that all was OK when she arrived. Mum wanted to tell her personally about the separation. It pained us all so very much. Then, not long after, dad gave mum an ultimatum to come home, or get divorced, as he would no longer be accepting of the separation. Mum insisted she needed more time, but to no avail. He went forward with the divorce, which truly devastated us. Ever since that first major breakdown I had held myself together.

How did I do that? I buried the emotions. I felt that it would be a betrayal to discuss my parents with anyone else. I started smoking. I drank more and more. I could lose myself to my social life and not think about what was happening at home. It was also when I was twenty, that my boyfriend promptly dropped me, to get married to the Afrikaans woman his parents approved of more than me, and with whom he had two-timed me for a long time. I was devastated. I felt unworthy, unloved, and empty. I ended up changing jobs, too, and got a good secretarial job at BP (British Petroleum) and lost myself to my work. Having a respectable job meant less parties and, in many ways, I settled down. I met a new boyfriend at work, and it became serious very quickly. The previous two years had been tumultuous and left me very unsteady, emotionally. Putting on a strong face and just "taking care of business" became my survival mechanism.

Dad had met my stepmother around that time, too. She made him incredibly happy. That was a good thing. What was hard was having to be the person to tell mum. It had only been a year since the divorce. Around that time, I got engaged to my then boyfriend. We celebrated our engagement at my 21st birthday party.

That engagement didn't work. Thank goodness. I broke it off, and moved back home, which was a common yo-yo pattern, with dad always ready to catch me. When I was twenty-two, I packed up all my possessions and moved myself to Cape Town. By then, I was a wreck, but nobody would guess. I was still smoking, drinking, and by then significantly overweight, too. It wasn't until my fifties when I learned the association of stress and depression to inflammatory diseases and weight gain. I also praise God that I never had any interest in drugs of any shape or form.

The reality is that moving cities, changing jobs, and even establishing a new lifestyle doesn't heal the pain. The problem is that *I was still there. We are the common denominator of our lives.*

The first job I had was a traveling salesperson selling jewellery. That simply did not work, and the final straw was when the boss/owner tried to force himself on me on frequent occasions. I finally quit and the days of having to pretend I wasn't home, came to an end. I had various casual relationships, including one-night stands, and often not sleeping at home. Instead, racing into shower and change to get the early train to work. I'd also hooked up with some loser who tried to introduce me to what we called "pot" – but it was obviously laced with something else, as it was the "trip of a lifetime" which left me so afraid and so disgusted with myself, that I never did it again. He dumped me, as did the next, and the next. I felt used. I felt unworthy, and I felt terribly alone. I felt that I was nothing more than a one-night stand and that I was not destined to find true love. I felt distanced from my family and had lied for so long about my lifestyle that I didn't like being with them anyway. It culminated in another breakdown, except that time, alone in my little flat, and having drunk a significant amount, I decided I didn't want to keep living any longer. I had shown signs of depression and the doctor obliged by giving me bottles of antidepressants and sleeping pills.

I overdosed. Then I was afraid and called a colleague's wife who rushed me to the hospital. I was required to engage in therapy after that, which I did, but by the time I'd gone back to my life, I'd neatly put all that emotion back into the "black box" (Dad's expression for what you did with things that shouldn't be remembered or spoken about.) I totally duped the therapist and went right back to my life. I never processed a thing.

Lesson One. When we deny the reality of an emotional wound, it will turn toxic.

It festered deep within me. I moved back to Johannesburg when I was promoted back to the company head office. I worked hard and played hard, while my career took off. I was very good at my job and have always had a successful career. In many ways, my career and my work life were my escape from the inner wounds. The safety of having to "have it all together" and succeed in my jobs were a haven from everything that happened after I left the office. Boyfriends came and went, and I continued to assuage the pain with temporary fixes and self-destructive habits. Anything would do, so long as it helped me keep that black box locked.

Several years after being back home, I was once again in a precarious state, emotionally. The wounds had turned toxic and now nothing helped. When I was still in Cape Town, I'd made a promise to the senior boss (married) that I would go out with him when he came to Johannesburg, in return for a favour he had done me. A class quid pro quo – a term I was to learn about in my human resources career many years later. He was a nice person and a good lover. The night he stood me up was on the heels of a lousy performance review at work that had just devastated me. I had always used my job as my escape and where I found self-worth. A bad performance review was a big enough trigger to have me spiralling and feeling anxious, tearful, and weak. I tried not to cry as I drove downtown to his hotel. I had to be strong. I also thought I should break it off anyway. I've never been in favour of dating a married man. What *was* I doing?!

Lesson Two. Never attach your sense of self-worth and identity to something as fickle as your job. Who we are is so much more than what we do.

As I left the hotel, having waited unsuccessfully for a while, I was in a state of utter despair. I drove home feeling numb, as I seemed to be past the tears. I hated myself, and thought again, I would never be loved. Now, I couldn't even succeed at work. That was the final blow. I swallowed the entire bottle of antidepressants on the nightstand. I'd started taking medications because the other methods were no longer helping. It was during the early stages of the trend that your doctor would just give you tablets to "take the edge off," or help you sleep, or reduce your depression without requiring any behavioural or mental health support. In those days, as it is sadly still today to some degree, diagnostics and prescriptions were the norm, rather than prevention and upstream solution seeking. I was still seeing our old family doctor who had treated us since we were little girls. He was a fatherly figure who would deal with many of my maladies, but never questioned me about my lifestyle, my choices, the messes I was getting myself into.

I woke up in the hospital and the first thought I had was extreme guilt. Who was I to have been so selfish as to put my family through such a terrible ordeal? My stepmother had found me and obviously I was not going to be done with my life any time soon. Les Brown, my mentor, once told a story about a man who had failed at a suicide attempt and recognised that God told him "It wasn't your life to take." That day, I had that realisation too, and knew two more. One was that I had caused my family terrible stress; and secondly, there had to be a better way to live. God planted a vision in my heart that day – to become a much better version of myself, and to help others do the same.

Lesson Three: No matter how big our mess, God will help us turn it into a message, if we give Him a chance. To have a testimony we must live through the test.

My life may feel great right now and, in many ways, I'm very blessed, but there was a long journey to getting here, with many twists and turns along the way. Rethinking myself was a process that I followed several times, and continue to follow, to get my life where I want it to be. I didn't always get it right and everything I've learned in that journey has now become my curriculum to empower others. My life's work is to help others live a life of purpose, passion, and power. That also means helping those with emotional wounds to recognise the reality of that and how to learn from it and grow through it, to become all that they are meant to be.

Even though God opened my eyes to a better life that day, I didn't immediately start doing what I needed to do. My life went on for several more years in the same rut of working hard and playing hard. The difference was that the old methods no longer gave me the same results because something had changed within me. I had what I now know as "divine discontent." I met a new boyfriend and I then got myself pregnant. Not the best of timing, but the blessing that came from that was immense. During the first few days of having to accept and live with what was such a moral "black mark" (to add to the already long list of reasons to hate myself) I heard some powerful words from a pastor I had reached out to. As I sat weeping, he held my hand and said, "God knew how much you needed someone to love and be loved. You tried to take your own life, but He's given you one in return." In that moment, I felt the grace, the love, the mercy, and the absolute peace that truly passes all understanding. I was at the feet of Jesus. I was face to face with grace, love, and a deep sense of joy.

From then until now, I have never taken another antidepressant. In step with Jesus, I began the process of rebuilding my life. I had to start over and rethink everything.

Since then, the only time I've done dumb things and got myself into messes, is when I've relegated Jesus to the passenger (or even the back) seat and taken back the steering wheel of my life. As maturity and wisdom have set in, those situations have become very rare, if at all. Something about landing face down in the mud to give you wisdom. I've fallen enough times to just not go near any mud piles and now happily accept riding shotgun. The ride is smooth and a heck of a lot more fun, too.

When my daughter was about three, I got married, and a few years later, we emigrated to the United States. My journey through that major life change was challenging, and just a few days before our flight to New York, I had a "Holy Spirit encounter" early one morning during prayer.

I had the incredible internal sense that God was going to do something hugely impactful with my life. I even spoke to my stepbrother about it at the time considering he was a pastor – they should know about these things, after all! He told me to trust the feeling, "Let go and let God." I guess in many ways I did, and I have; but not until I made a mighty mess of things during my divorce and the early years in my own business.

Lesson Four: Even after we trust God, we will still mess up, because we are not perfect. Life is more a series of detours, backtracks, and re-directs, than a perfect upward slope.

We can be slow learners at times, especially when our pride and ego get in the way. Years ago, I heard an apt saying, that "ego" meant "edging God out." That's exactly what it did. Our emigration brought a whole new level of stress, adjustment, and loneliness, as I'd left my entire family back in South Africa. I had to adjust to having no job, no status, no friends, and in-laws who didn't exactly love me or my daughter. By then, I had started the hard work on myself, rethinking things and finding that when I centred myself and focused on my strengths, I was able to start a successful coaching practice and make significant friendships with those who resonated with my talents and my life purpose. Being around people who build you up more than tear you down is an important part of getting yourself back together.

As I was drawn into my work and this new network, my husband was more and more distant. He spent time away from home, with people I didn't know, and would often disappear for an entire weekend. I was devastated as I watched our marriage slowly come apart, just as I'd watched happen with my parents. The difference was that I was stronger, and clearer headed. I know that while every marriage takes two people one way or another, I had perhaps married the wrong person. Our lives were on separate tracks. He resented and often openly criticised my friends and the people I worked with.

I tried one final time to put things back together and planned a vacation to our timeshare. At the last minute, he pulled out, saying he had pressures and work and couldn't leave. My daughter and I went alone, only to have a good friend and neighbour tell me after the fact that there had been another woman at the house with him. I realised I had a decision to make. His family owned the house. I had taken everything I'd owned (including my own house, purchased when my daughter was just eighteen months old) into this marriage. I would leave with nothing. We would be totally alone. I could do that. I believed in myself. My daughter by then was nearly thirteen, and when I told her that rainy Thanksgiving weekend (after another night waiting for him and crying my heart out) that we were going to find an apartment, she was very happy. Turns out, she'd been walking the path I had walked at eighteen, watching your parents' marriage breakup in front of you.

We went to South Africa that Christmas, and it was arranged that we would move into the apartment when we got back. Through it all I convinced myself that I was fine, and totally in control. My daughter and I made the tough decision that we would not return to South Africa, where we had our entire family and everything we loved. Instead, we knew that to stay in the USA was the right thing to do, even though it would be hard. It was. We survived, but only recently have I become aware of the terrible toll on my daughter's emotional health and what is now chronic anxiety.

I worked hard (don't I always?) and at times, it was the credit card that paid the bills when I couldn't. My consulting work was a roller coaster – feast or famine – which didn't bode well for my financial health. I engaged in a wild online dating life during the early days of AOL chat rooms, and made some disastrous decisions related to the type of people I engaged with. And again, one morning it just suddenly hit me. I looked at myself in the mirror, and spoke to myself firmly – this is *not* who I am. This is *not* the life God saved me for. I recognised, too, that I had a responsibility to my daughter and was not a good role model. So, just a few months after we'd left my husband, I stopped all the "bad behaviour" and focused on my business, learning, and church.

Once my daughter was finished with middle school, we left the costly west Los Angeles area and moved south closer to San Diego – what they call "North County." There, we found our footing. We settled in a wonderful church, she had a great group of friends and loved her high school, which was directly adjacent to the apartments we lived in. I soon landed a really good, secure job, and despite having to go through a bankruptcy, and later the voluntary foreclosure on a town home I'd purchased during the crash of 2008, I was able to slowly rebuild my finances and sense of self.

Lesson Five: Recognise when you need to get out of an environment that is not healthy

Today, just ten years since the move out of Los Angeles, I am thriving and living a life of joy, purpose, and focus. Let me focus my story now on what has unfolded in my life since and share with you that I have learned about putting myself together and staying on the right track.

I had originally developed a program called *"The Third Alternative"* in those early days of arrival in the USA and had even done a speaking tour back in South Africa in the mid-nineties. The original idea and outline had been written before we left South Africa. That had sparked something in me. Combined with my experience gained from my successful consulting work, I recognised that I had the ability to positively impact the lives of other people. It slowly took shape, and I invested time and money in my own development.

The work that I took with that company in north county San Diego, though, soon took over all my time as I expanded into more roles at an executive level. It was right for us at the time. Being a single parent, I found that the stability of steady employment, company benefits, and continued experience was a strong attraction. My own business was the price I had to pay. You can't easily be employed and build a business – well at least, I didn't think so at the time. I worked too hard to have any margin left for creative development of my gifts and skills.

My daughter went on to college, got her degree, and moved back home. She worked at the same company as I did for a while, and soon we relocated to Colorado Springs, where we still live.

The years briefly summarised above were a chapter of my life that felt like a long detour off the track of living my purpose. My personal mission has always been to empower others to be the best they can be at who they are meant to be. Now I know that everything I learned from that job, and subsequent consulting gigs in the past several years, have strengthened my skill set and given me extremely important skills and experiences. More than ever, my work with others through coaching and training (my true passion) brings me deep joy and I am finally living the life of my dreams.

Lesson Six: No experience or event in your life is ever wasted.

There is a powerful worship song by Gungor called "Beautiful Things." God makes beautiful things out of the dust, out of us. All my self-inflicted mistakes and wrong turns, He gently pulled back out of the quagmires and dead-ends I'd created and re-directed into the person I am today. How things will ultimately work for your good is not always visible or perceivable when you go through those setbacks. My coach says, "You can't see the picture when you're in the frame," and I was recently given that quote in an impromptu speaker event where I had five minutes to speak on it. It was perfect. I couldn't have asked for a better prompt because that is what I've lived in the past twenty-one years since my divorce. The best times of my development were when I engaged in learning and got help from coaches, teachers, mentors.

Lesson Seven: You can't be objective enough about your own life in order to re-shape it, on your own. It's important to get help.

In my current business, I am a thinking coach. I help people to remap the thinking patterns in their brains that are causing outward successes or failures. Our behaviour is the outward expression of our thoughts and emotions, which are the result of beliefs and assumptions (the operating systems) of our subconscious mind that have been created as a result of all our life experiences. God may upcycle the junk, but it's up to you and me to upcycle the thinking that created the messes. Build on what makes sense, re-program what doesn't.

In recent months, as I step out on larger stages and build expanded audiences, I have told and retold my story several times. At first it was difficult. I had successfully buried much of my experience, having healed my mind and my heart. Then I appreciated that my life is a story to tell to empower others (like you the reader) to establish health and fulfilment in their lives, no matter how big their messy piles of junk are!

All my years in corporate training have honed my skills as a trainer, facilitator, and content developer. I love to create programs and tools, resources, and lessons that equip people to develop what they need to, to live fully empowered and exponential lives. That old program, *"The Third Alternative"* brought together the foundational pieces to what is now the anchor program of ReThink You. The new program called, *"You: Inside-Out – A 6-week Journey of Transformation,"* is the culmination of the past thirty plus years of learning, experiencing, healing, and growing. This is what I was saved to do. I have also created a six-month *Exponential Living* Program that brings all the tools into an integrated journey where I walk alongside a person for six months as they go through three key phases of development. My journey to wholeness and to a place of living my purpose followed these phases and the way I am uniquely designed compels me to take whatever I learn and make it teachable to others.

Too many times when a person is considering what they are meant to do in life, they tend to overlook, diminish, or even ignore their natural talents and strengths. Don't try to be all things to all people. Don't try to do what everyone else thinks you should do. Observe yourself. Evaluate yourself. Look at what you've done, whether good or bad, and what you have learned along the way. That is the start of your journey to what you should be doing, and along the way, you become the very best version of yourself.

REGROUP

This is the first step toward getting away from any feelings of hopelessness and self-deprecation. The analogy I use is that of driving on the freeway and feeling lost, anxious, panicky. Pull off the road. Stop. Think. Regroup.

At every juncture of my life when I "pulled myself up" it was a process of taking stock. Looking at my life and evaluating what was wrong or right about it. Results don't lie. Whatever you are experiencing is the result of your thinking, feelings, and behaviour. When I was in debt, and not generating enough business to keep us afloat, my wake-up call was when God sent a check for just $293.75 in the mail, which was the exact amount I needed for a bill. I don't remember the source of the money, not do I remember what bill needed paying, but I remember the day, the moment, the image of that check imprinted in my brain. I think it was His way of reminding me who should have been holding the steering wheel. I felt ashamed and guilty. He was faithful and reliable, but I had not been acting responsibly.

Regroup can be done if you're self-aware enough to be honest and own your mistakes. I did. I wrote down everything that I didn't like about my life. Then, I wrote down all the things that I wanted, and what I loved about my life. The regroup process is a reckoning of past, present, and future. It's taking stock of your life, and who you have become in the process. It's identifying the incorrect thinking and behaviours, writing them down, and examining the reasons for them. For me it was also necessary to examine the reasons behind my depression and downward spiral. At times, we need help. This is where those early therapy sessions were highly valuable. If you are considering therapy, I encourage you to consider it as a necessary step out of whatever you are dealing with. That said, be sure that your therapist is there to help you regroup, and not let you stay in the "mud," with endless re-telling of the same stories. Talk therapy is only helpful (in my opinion) when it is focused on moving forward and taking the lessons from the past. Otherwise, if you are just talking about all the stuff of life, you are not progressing.

My early studies (during that fateful one year at university) included Psychology. I also engaged in training in Christian counselling soon after my divorce, and in recent years, have pursued learning more about neurobiology, neuroscience, and well-established practices in cognitive behavioural therapy. As a thinking coach, I help individuals re-map their sub-conscious thinking patterns – those "levers" of behaviour that take you toward or away from what you really desire in life. I say all this to say that I'm not a stranger to the world of psychotherapy and behavioural health methodologies. I have found that when an individual is ready to do the work of rebuilding their thinking, traditional talk therapy is no longer the best option. Coaching is a better option. Find what you need – but regroup and take stock of your life with honesty and compassion for the you of your past.

The regroup process also includes figuring out what you want. Knowing what you want is critically important, because if you don't form a clear sense of who you want to be and what you want to do, what you don't want will continue to fill the vacuum. The universe, nature, God's design, abhors a vacuum. We are designed to live in balance, in homeostasis. Remove the negative, the toxic, and unhelpful, from your life, and be ready to fill it with the positive, growth-oriented, and life-giving new behaviours, thoughts, emotions, and desires. That takes some work, and it takes time, and it's the second phase of getting yourself on track.

Steps you can take right now:

- ✓ If you don't yet journal, this exercise may be a way to start what is a helpful practice to improve life balance and a sense of peace. Write down as much of your life story as you can. Write your own "chapter" or even an entire book. But writing it down gives you a clearer perspective.
- ✓ Look for the highs and lows in the story. What can you build on? What do you think you should let go? What would that look like?
- ✓ Think about what triggers you into depression or lack of self-worth. Write that down under the heading, "What I don't want." Then,

under the heading, "What I do want," write down what is the complete opposite. If it was working well, what would that look like? How can you take immediate steps toward what you do want?
✓ Take some time to write out your dreams and desires. What is it you genuinely want in life?

REFRAME

When you are done regrouping, before you think of getting back on the "road of life," it is important to reframe your narrative.

In the current era, the younger generation have not had the experience of living with tape recorders, whether spooled or cassette. Recognising that, I will take a different approach to unpacking why reframing is such a critical aspect of rethinking yourself. You see, as you go through all your life experiences, your brain is recording the narratives, the internal "code" that drives your emotional response, and then the outward behaviour to match. The more you repeat a narrative (aka your stories) the more entrenched the pattern in the brain. When "A" happens, the brain responds with "B." Here's what that sounds like: "That's just the way I am." Or "That's how I've always been." Or "It runs in my family – my father was the same." Or "As I get older, the more I am like my mother."

Resonate with any of that? Then you understand what it is to have the same tracks running on a repeat loop throughout your life. Therapy followed by cognitive and neuroscientific coaching can help you hit the pause or stop button, and re-record. You can, and absolutely must, reframe the narratives that keep you stuck in loops of unhelpful emotions and behaviours.

Here's another truth I learned when I started the reframe process in my own life: Your brain can make mistakes, or even tell downright lies. (The reason eye-witness testimony is so unreliable.) If your short-term memory has some "blanks" the brain will fill the blank space with learned memory from its storage, which is significantly large. It will remember data points from any number of historical events. It makes mistakes and sometimes will choose an incorrect data point – pushing out what becomes "virus code" in the system.

Some examples of virus code thinking include:

"People always let me down."

"If I make a mistake, people will not forgive me."

"I feel rejected if people don't respond to my ideas with encouragement."

"I don't like sharing too much – people always throw it back in my face."

"I avoid confrontation because I don't want people to think less of me."

"I am not worthy of success."

I was fortunate that around the time I was regrouping my life, I encountered a professional who had mastered the art of reframing. It is his method I use to this day to help others. No matter what source you find for yourself, the important step is to reframe. Wherever you go, there you are. So, if things are not working out in your life, start with you, which is all that you can truly control.

Regrouping and reframing were the foundations of me rebuilding my life and then showing others how to do the same. Here's the important lesson – they must be repeated at various times. It's not a "one and done" process. Life is constantly in flux. Circumstances change. Newly learned thinking patterns can get forgotten when not reinforced and you could find yourself back in virus code. Your goals may have been achieved and you're ready for what's next. You are a work in progress, and I knew that constant personal development was essential if I was to create a life of success. So, the third phase of rethinking you is that of refocusing.

Steps you can take right now:

- ✓ Using the same journal as before, examine and write down the narratives that you have used within yourself either alone, or when you speak to others.
- ✓ What labels have you given yourself? How will you reframe that to more closely match what you know to be true of yourself right now? What changes need to happen to the narrative to support what you want?

- ✓ When you are stressed, depressed, hopeless, who can you reach out to for support, encouragement, and empathetic listening? Ask them to help you reframe so you can see a new perspective.
- ✓ Consider finding yourself a coach!
- ✓ Commit to taking just one small step in the next twenty-four hours.

REFOCUS

When you have reframed, only then can you focus forward and focusing forward is critical. The previous step of reframing will most likely take away the sense of panic, the anxiety and the hopelessness. It did for me then, as it does now. You can then get back on "the road" of your life and start heading in the direction toward what you really want. You will also be better off if you spend more time looking through the windscreen as you drive back onto the road and direct yourself to your desired destination, than remaining focused on the rear-view mirror.

This phase is also one that I go through at least every year, and at times, every few months. Refocus is about setting direction and putting the plans into place to get to where you have decided you are going. It amazes me how many people avoid any form of goal setting and instead choose to live in the land of pipe dreams where the random ideas float, the desires to do better become like fleeting thoughts like the small clouds in the sky – constantly shifting, but never producing rain. People don't plan to fail. They fail to plan.

I will say less about this because this phase is commonly explained in other resources. Google "personal life planning" and you will be inundated with tools. My point is that it is fun, even exhilarating to refocus on a regular basis if, and only if, you are in a healthy place of balance and self-awareness. You have let go what doesn't work. You have a healthy sense of what you want in life and how you can get it. Shed the old, before you can plan the new.

Steps you can take right now:

- ✓ Write down at least one significant goal for each area of your life. These are goals that will result in you getting closer to what you want.
- ✓ Find some personal planning tools to keep yourself on track toward a better future.
- ✓ Take one small step toward a goal in the next twenty-four hours.

IN CLOSING

As you go through life, think of yourself as a train. The destination sometimes changes, and you go onto different routes, but along the way you have multiple station stops – each one representing a chapter of life. I've shared several of my stations with you in this chapter. As you complete a station stop – whether a career, a relationship, a painful event, a joyful event – you are ready to leave the station and continue your journey. But your train doesn't take baggage, it only carries passengers. The passengers that board your train at the station are the lessons - the takeaways that will make the journey ahead more powerful, more fruitful, and the positive emotions that resulted from the "station stop." The baggage is negative emotion and self-deprecation. The baggage are the feelings of anger, regret, bitterness, guilt, shame. If you acquiesce and allow that baggage on your train, you will run out of space for new passengers.

Over all these years of constant rethinking, I've discovered the importance of holding onto the lessons and the happy memories and moving past toxic negativity. Harbouring grudges, holding on to anger, living a life of resentment – all contribute to keeping me stuck in places I don't want to be. I've been in some pretty ugly places in my journey, and I don't want to go back there ever again. So, it's up to me to take responsibility for my mental health, my mindset, my behaviours. I know what I want, and I am enjoying the journey toward that!

At times, it feels like an exceptionally long time since I woke up in that hospital bed. But when I look at the memories of the train journey so far, I realise that it has been a few chapters of learning, and a whole lot of personal development, accountability, and ownership to bring me to where I am now. I still regroup, reframe, refocus, to keep myself firmly on the tracks of my train ride toward what I truly desire in life. I've just found it gets easy to avoid the routes I know will take me off course, and every passenger I choose to keep on for the ride has helped me become the version of myself I always knew I could be. I believe in myself now. I live each day with a joyful sense of expectation that comes from a place of healed self-awareness. It's what I want for you, too. I hope that sharing my story and my lessons will prove to be a powerful "station stop" for your train, too.

REFLECTIONS

REFLECTIONS

REFLECTIONS

Neringa Brand

Neringa Branisauskaite is a Guide & an Energy Healer at Shakti Essence. First time Author, sharing her story about overcoming suicidal thoughts & how healing helped her retire from the Sex Industry. She's seeking to educate the Youth about the reality of Sex & Adult Industries. Also, to help women with their marriages through the wisdom she's gained during eleven years of sex & adult work.

Grief As The Saving Grace

BY NERINGA BRANISAUSKAITE
UK

Growing up I felt like I didn't belong. To my surprise, the older I get the less I remember about my childhood; or if I do remember, the memories are very negative, and I find it impossible to find the positives.

The trauma I have endured daily has taken away the ability to remember. I truly hated my life. It felt like my existence was a chore to my parents. I felt like I was a burden, and probably that stems from my arrival on the physical plane. My mum still reminds me of the traumatic experience she endured during labour. From her stories I was not too keen to leave my mother's womb. The birth took twenty-four hours, I had an umbilical cord around my neck and the memory now feels like I was coming out with my right shoulder which I feel is quite significant as it is a masculine side of the body, and you will find out what it had to do with my life later down the line.

The birth trauma has definitely impacted my life. I was born a redhead and that brought a lot of difficulties just like the birth itself. No one ever told me growing up how special redheads are, and that only 1% of humans on the planet are blessed with this striking physical feature, which led to me getting bullied.

It began pretty much the first day I stepped into a nursery at the age of three years old. I was made aware pretty rapidly that I was not in the prettiest girls' squad in my class and that I should just be quiet and hide. Yet my personality was so bright and loud, I did not follow the rules of these children's cruel society. However, it did begin the lifelong suppression of my character. I understood that wherever I went I would be frowned upon; that I am not like everyone else, that I was not pretty, and that the freckles on my face were some sort of skin problem I will never be able to get rid of. I was doomed, for life.

I stayed away from the sun so my freckles wouldn't get any brighter and looked into the bleaching creams as I wished for my face to be clear, so I could get a bronze tan like the pretty girls in the nursery. I wanted to have blonde hair and look like the popular girls.

Learning during the lessons had never been my top priority because I felt so different, so unloved, and ridiculed. All the pain of not belonging and the cruel experiences at home made me look for love as soon as I could write.

To be loved by a boy was my main goal and I chased that in every opportunity I could get. I would love someone new every week. My 'love' was quite possessive. That week's lucky boy received a love letter in the nursery's lockers, only to get rejected every time. I was pretty determined to have a boyfriend. With every rejection I got more obsessed with unfathomable need to be chosen. I was a joke in my class, no boy really took me seriously and all they did was laugh, call me names, and reiterate the fact that I was not worthy. I was not worthy of a boy's love.

I grew up believing that I did not deserve to have what everyone else had. Ever since I was six years old, I have had an inner knowing that the guy I would love the most will die because that was to be expected from my life, because all the bad things happened to me.

So many times, I wondered why I was born at all, and I felt it would be so much easier for me to just die. I envisioned my death so many times and I was only about six years old. I saw myself getting hit by a car numerous times, but that seemed to be too painful. Then I would imagine taking loads of pills from my grandparent's impressive medicine cabinet. Each time the guilt was too much because I knew that if I did this, at least one person would suffer and that was my Nana. I didn't want to do that to her, so I continued my suffering. My nana was the hero in my story because she suffocated me with her love and that's exactly what I needed. I then realised how manipulative and traumatic that love had been because she kept asking me how I would feel if she and my grandpa died. This would make me go into overwhelming anxiety and fear, as if my fear and tears were some sort of validation for her existence.

I was always a little princess for my grandpa and grandma, and I felt like they loved me more than they loved my mum - which I secretly loved and thought it was her karma because mum didn't love me. My grandparents really were a safe haven for me.

The overwhelming feeling of not belonging came from not receiving the love that I needed from my mother and father. My mum had me when she was twenty-one and so her life was very busy, and it felt like there was no time for me. She excelled at being a great student and an employee, so that did not leave much capacity for the emotional support a toddler would require. My dad was in the Soviet Army and has been an alcoholic for as long as I can remember. Seeing him sober was like a special occasion, but those special occasions would only make him drink even more, leaving me with nothing from either parent.

My parents' inability to connect with each other in a healthy manner created two very fearful monsters in my young mind. Both were as bad as each other with the abuse, which from what I can remember was quite constant. As the years went by, the abuse intensified. The most feared object dad used to hit us with was a white leather army belt with metal studs on, and it wasn't just a few strikes either. It was a full-blown attack; about six to ten strikes minimum. He really put his back into it; my legs and butt were bruised for weeks. That's the way he disciplined my brother and I while we were still quite small. As soon as I grew up, the abuse took a different turn.

When I was born, I was 'Daddy's girl' but somehow that love turned into hate maybe because I continuously asked mum to divorce him. He blamed me for their divorce for many years.

I was about twelve years old when I looked death closely in the eye. It felt like it was my last day on this planet. Dad asked me to come back from my grandparents at a specific time, because he wanted the house to be warm by setting up a fireplace. I came back two hours early, and in his rage, in the kitchen, he punched me in the stomach. I remember thinking "Finally my suffering will end. I just want to die". I believed he did this because he hated me, and it was best for me to be dead. After the beating he was frantic and kept repeating 'breathe, breathe, breathe, please I am sorry, breathe'. Even though I caught my breath, and he swiftly changed his tune, it was too late. No apology could have changed the way I felt, and something happened in that moment that broke me fully and I could never ever respect my father again.

Mum had a strategy which terrified my brother and me. Every time we misbehaved, and most of the time simply because she lacked patience, she would slap us both at the same time with the back of her hands. There were so many occasions that it was inexcusable the way she would hit us for the littlest things, but the abuse reached its panache much later in my life.

I left my parents' home to live with my grandparents after the punching incident. Even though I spent a lot of time with my grandparents, that day was the final straw and I refused to be in my dad's presence again and refused him as my guardian.

My parents' abuse continued, it was an on/off battle, just like their entire marriage. I have escaped the physical abuse but not the emotional trauma which continued for many years to come.

The next stage of abuse began when I was fourteen years old because I did not know my mum anymore after she left us to work in England. My most significant abandonment happened when she left Lithuania looking for a better life and running away from my crazy, alcoholic father. When I was fifteen years old mum moved my brother and I to England. A year later, after experiencing so many mum's anger episodes which resulted in more physical abuse, I was met with my worst abuse yet, I was almost raped.

The house we lived in, in Leeds, had many lodgers, about ten at that time. A man who lived on the first floor with his partner and new-born sneaked up on me sleeping in a bed with another flatmate. He told my mum and this revelation was a direct indication that I was having sex, in her house, with her tenant. The rage she was in took over her and she beat me up on New Year's Day, a few weeks after my sixteenth birthday.

Mum's partner at the time and two other drunken men watched her drag me by the hair on the floor and get kicked numerous times. After that, her partner forced me and one of my friends to look down his pants at his cock whilst degrading me for having had sex at my age. As my mum left to take my friend home, she turned around and said to the men 'Do whatever you want with this whore'. I thought that was going to be the end of me and that I wouldn't come out of this alive or in one piece.

The youngest guy took the initiative and was very close to raping me, but I kept fighting him off as much as I possibly could, while he destroyed everything in my room, smashing my wardrobe's mirror, pulling clothes and everything he got his hands on out on the floor. He tried everything, but I was never going to give up this fight. I kept thinking I cannot be one of the girls who get raped like this, I just cannot. I kept praying for a miracle. The rape was prevented by my best friend's dad. He came to the rescue, trying to protect me from the main abuser by getting me in bed with him, groping me and telling me how he's going to save me if I just stayed in bed with him and kept still. Eventually what felt like a few hours mum got back, and tried to stop all the carnage, but during this chaos, finally realizing what she's done, she tried to stop the men, but instead got beaten up by her partner. Meanwhile the man, who told her, robbed the entire house.

The traumas I have shared so far are the ones I can remember the most. All these experiences led me into a life of shame, grief, pain and rejection. I chose and attracted men who loved and wanted my body, but not much more. I was very needy and very broken; I would describe myself as more fragile than fragile itself. Not having much luck in the relationship department, except my most normal relationship at the age of twenty-one, but since then I have never been able to get a guy to commit to a relationship. I call this one my lucky, happiest and most normal relationship thus far.

When I was eighteen years old, I went on a date with a woman to have 'no strings attached fun' with her. However, the purpose of this date wasn't what I thought it was. It was a glimpse of hope, a glimpse of financial independence and an escape from the industrial factory work that I had despised since the legal working age in the UK.

She showed me the ropes of the Adult work website, details on how to use the set up to work at home as a webcam model. I felt like I had won a lottery. As I always dread the thought of being stuck in the factory, grafting away without any real prospects. I always felt like I was meant for more and this was it!

The excitement and eagerness to earn and be seen as a model was so appealing to me. I was so turned on by the thought of being watched, and it was my secret, it empowered me and scared me at the same time. The fake sense of self-esteem and power grew the more I worked on webcam. Half a year into my business, my laptop broke. I was terrified to lose my independence and financial security. There was no other way for me to get a laptop but to turn to escorting. I promised myself it's only once, it's only to get the laptop so I can stay safe at home and carry on webcamming. My first client was a guy who spent big money on me during those first months of my career on webcam, he talked me into meeting him. The curiosity and desperation led me to him. He was triple my age and I was so disgusted by him. I had no feelings for him and felt so repulsed by the perversion of it all and that I just sold my soul for £500.

I got black out drunk to numb myself from what I had just gotten myself into; the man was pretty terrifying when he was on top of me. I was so drunk I could not even look at him. I had my eyes closed the whole time, not that I could see much due to the haze of the alcohol. I am sure he felt just as bad as I did. He did not leave a review nor contact me again. It was embarrassing and shocking for us both. He wanted a fresh, unspoiled pussy, and he really got to feel what a nineteen-year-old newbie escort felt like, and no surprises here but for me it felt like molestation.

I cried for days, I felt so dirty, so unworthy. I felt like I could never tell what happened to anyone because they would judge me. However, the desperation at the time was more intense than the disgust. I was pleased and relieved when I got a new laptop. It meant that I could forget how I got the laptop and carry on with my little webcam venture.

I was twenty-two years old when I met a male porn star who persuaded me to move to another city and start escorting full time because I was young and pretty and I had to use my assets to make loads of money otherwise it would just be a waste. With no help from him, as if by miracle I found a two bedroom flat days before I had to move, and just like that I started my escorting career full time. I started off by charging ridiculously low prices for my services and so I met clients who saw me as trash and wanted me to give them more than what they were paying for.

I hated that so much but most of the time I complied because that is what I was used to my entire life. Although I was definitely not forced into anything I was persuaded to do many things that I did not want to do.

At this point I started consuming large amounts of coke to deal with the grief of my grandpa who died when I was seventeen and the near rape experience. Before the drugs I was not processing my feelings as I did not really talk about it sober. Coke helped me or so I thought to process the harsh reality about my mum allowing me to almost get raped and telling them to do whatever they wanted with me. I simply could not understand how that could happen to me, so I used large amounts of drugs to numb the pain and silence the chaos that experience created within me.

The summer of the first escorting year I went to my first festival with escort friends. It was an awful experience because they kept leaving me and it was the first time, I had been outside feeling so high. I was not having a good time and ended up taking a lot of ecstasy pills from a dealer who appeared out of nowhere. He encouraged me to take as many of it as I wanted. It was the second time I had taken 'pills' and I thought it wasn't working. After a handful of ecstasy and some coke, known as a 'pills bomb', I found myself going through an experience that I would never wish on anyone.

Not knowing what was going on, I found myself at a friend's apartment for the after party and I did not know what to do with myself. I lay down on the floor because I could not stand on my feet. I did not want to be in a room full of strangers. Then suddenly I felt extremely cold, so I got in bed. That made me feel very hot and sweaty as if I was very sick. I repeatedly went on the floor and got back into bed. I thought I was losing the plot; nothing was making sense, why was I feeling like this? Luckily, I managed to get a cab home and then it dawned on me that I had overdosed. After all, I took insane amounts of unknown pills, coke and MDMA.

The four days which followed were so scary. I could not sleep. The nightmares, the night tremors, the spinning of the room, the visions of demons, were unbearable. I was stuck in bed. I could not move; I had no food and only managed sips of water for the duration of that time. I was terrified but had nothing to lose so I called my mum and told her that I might be dying. I told her that I do not understand what's going on with my brain and body. My head felt like I was squeezed from every corner of the brain. I could not see; I could not move.

My mum handled the situation pretty well with only a few passive aggressive comments. I am truly grateful for her support, otherwise, I would not have gotten myself to the shop to get some fruit and herbal antidepressants. As soon as I ate some watermelon and took a few 'Kalms' 'the herbal antidepressants, I began my recovery. The entire comedown took about seven days, I later got told by the friend who was at the after party, that I had left just in time because as soon as I left someone ended up getting stabbed. I counted myself lucky, overdose is better than being stabbed. On the seventh day I was back at the bar with a Martini in my hand, clearly not having learned the lesson. A similar event repeated a year later.

These memories remind me how much I wanted to die, and even though I have never consciously tried to kill myself, unconsciously I chased the dragon to death. If there were ten grams of coke on the table, I would be the one to consume it all, and if there was more, I'd happily take that too. Most of the time I'd be in so much pain, the muscles and bones would be giving up on me, but I'd carry on until I had nothing left in me.

These benders were a normal part of life when I moved to London a year after the overdose incident. It was filled with filthy, kinky sex with my fuck buddy who was an escort too. He would steal loads of coke from his Arab client for us to have parties which would last for days and include loads of sex. Whenever I wanted to let my hair down, I just had to make an appointment with him, as he was so busy with escorting and entertaining other women.

Eventually the time came for a rude awakening when I started questioning things and got told he had a fiancé and that was one thing I could not tolerate as he lied to me continuously to keep me. I was fine with him working with other ladies but was not going to participate in our dance if he was in a committed relationship. My toxic fantasy has shattered into pieces, and a new one began the next morning.

By this point I had been escorting for nearly a decade, but I hadn't been to a proper Halloween party as I always partied indoors. For a month or so before the party on the 20th October I knew that I needed to be dressed as Snow White for this party. I had cried the entire day after finding out that my fuck buddy has lied to me for over three years, but I was determined to go. I had my makeup done professionally while keeping myself spaced out on coke. Feeling numb the entire time we went to the party. It was not enjoyable, but I knew I would meet someone that night; the inner knowing was just that this is IT, I will meet THE ONE. I knew that from the heartbreak I have just experienced something good has to come out of it.

I was on my way out, heading for the exit, when my eyes met these gorgeous green eyes (contact lenses) and that was IT! I knew in my entire being who he was. It was HIM, I have been waiting my whole life for him, since nursery, he was the one I was searching for! He knew me as well, we smiled, had a cheeky flirtatious conversation, exchanged numbers. It was the most romantic meeting I have ever experienced in my life. That was my story, my fairy tale.

What followed was not so romantic. Instead of meeting him when he was available, I was stroppy and followed my friend's advice to play hard to get for about 2 weeks, but that did not work on him. He wasn't playing my silly games, so eventually I gave up on that farce and booty called him for sex. I was too drunk and too in love to care about my reputation as I wanted him with my entire body and soul. He felt like the oxygen that I could breathe for the years to come.

Our first sexual encounter felt like I had come back home, the feeling of belonging, being one, souls merging, bodies uniting after lifetimes of separation. That was the feeling I was trying to find everywhere I turned. My story had a huge twist of faith when I told him that my best friend stalked him and found out a lot of information about him online. Things changed, he became more distant than usual, I had to wait for his message for weeks.

I had invited him to celebrate my twenty-seventh birthday with me, but he went to another party instead. I later found out that he had gone to the party with his ex. I excused his inconsistent behaviour and 10 days of disappearing acts because I realised that he partied all the time. He was high for most of his life. He prided himself on the number of parties and drugs he'd had. Showing off at the fact he mixed all the drugs together; coke, pills, ketamine, MDMA, GHB. He thought he was special because he was able to chase the dragon without any consequences. During our last time together, he showed me that he was a functioning addict as he took GHB, commonly known as the 'date rape' drug daily. I witnessed him having night tremors, choking, he couldn't breathe, and it was terrifying.

That night I realised that if I stayed with him, I would probably become a drug addict too and I made peace with it, as long as I was able to be with him. All his partying was masking the huge pain he has inherited when his mum set the house on fire when he was eight years old with him and two of his brothers in it. Stephen was the only one to survive after a gas explosion blew him out of the house through a window. The burden of his entire family leaving him, weighed heavily on him. So, the only way to survive was to numb himself at every opportunity he got.

At the end of January 2018, I went back to Lithuania to see my grandma, as I had not seen her for six years; I felt that it might be the last time I see her. She had dementia and her memories of me had vanished. She thought I was her mother when I visited her. That had a significantly negative effect on me because she brought me up, so I saw her more as a mother than a grandma. When I got back to London a week later, I did my best to manage my emotions and went on another adventure. As you may have guessed, it involved a lot of coke.

During that time, I got the courage to contact Stephen and ask him why he'd been so distant and has not communicated with me since my birthday in early December. He was online and did not react to any of my attempts to get him to talk, so I threatened him by saying I would come over. When he did not say anything, I went to his flat. I am glad I did because he finally expressed how he felt and told me in his way that he loved me. However, that was also the end of us.

The pain and grief I endured pushed me further down into the white powder, which I had plenty of as I stayed at my friend's flat where I was supposed to escort, and as he was a drug dealer, I went through a huge stash of his coke. I took at least six grams and I carried on for another 10 or so hours.

I was devastated with what happened between me and Stephen because my fairy tale was over before it had even started. With the help of alcohol and coke I managed to survive the heartbreak by working. Sometimes I was able to keep my emotions in check and other times having a breakdown on the clients. On the 16th February Stephens's Instagram announced that he had proposed to his ex-girlfriend. That announcement picture was for me. It was revenge. He knew I would see it because he thought I was a stalker. Fair to say I was obsessed, and I looked at his Instagram often. We had a very strong telepathic bond, so I knew what he was doing.

I remember feeling like I was in hell, going deeper into despair, howling my pain away in hope it would lessen, but it didn't. The only feeling that intensified was the desire to drink, do drugs and try to numb this horrific pain I was feeling. This habit was getting out of control and became very costly. It was a dangerous game I played once, twice, sometimes three times a week to bury my emotions so I wouldn't have to feel the continuous anxiety and negative thoughts. I kept hoping for Stephen to wake up and choose me, but he was way too deep in it with his fiancé and the drug addiction.

In 2018 almost a year after meeting me, he chose to take his own life and overdosed. The times where I was losing the will to live faded in comparison to this one. The love of my life was dead. I felt guilty about his death for so long because I felt responsible. I thought it was my fault because I did not chase him. I kept thinking I could have done more; I could have gone to the parties where he was at and spoken to him, told him that we can get through his pain and find a way out of his suffering. It felt as though I'd abandoned him. I knew that I was the braver one because I was able to express my feelings better than him and that I could have done more to help him to ease the pain he was in for so many years. I did not know any of his friends and by a miraculous synchronicity one of his good friends was on my Facebook page.

As soon as I saw her status "A couple passed away one after another". I knew that he and his fiancé were dead, yes, just like Romeo & Juliet. A few days prior to seeing this Facebook status Stephen was with me in a dream, and I knew that something wasn´t right; I felt that he could be dead, and then I discovered he was.

Attending the funeral is where I connected with his circle of friends. The tragedy of losing Stephen spiralled me out of control. I was looking for Stephen in other men, so I slept with one of his acquaintances and the pattern started to form. I partied a lot and got involved with men who used me physically, financially and emotionally. I was so toxic myself that the only men I was attracted to, were the equally toxic ones.

My situation worsened. I was high almost every day as I was seeing one of Stephen's friends and he was a drug dealer and the worst influence. I promised myself to change from the 22nd February – Stephen's birthday.

On that day I had my first Bufo Alvarius ceremony. Bufo is a toad that secretes 5-DMT Tryptamine, which is also produced naturally in the pineal gland in the brain while we are sleeping. Bufo Alvarius is a medicine formed by nature. My first dose was a 'hero dose' which is a big dose to unblock the brain from the trauma. I started changing. Toxic men who only wanted me to satisfy their needs were not for me anymore. I had outgrown that pattern which had been ingrained in me because of my childhood traumas. I was no longer a people pleaser.

The third ceremony was my resurrection. Yes, I know sounds insane, but it literally was. I had a dream that confirmed that I was going through a resurrection, my dreams were so vivid, I was going through Bufo trips pretty much every night. It was awesome, I was living for these dreams. I googled: How many days did the resurrection take in the Bible? It said three So, after three days I decided that I was healed. I thought, I can have a drink at my escort job that I had on a Friday evening. The guy took me to a lobster restaurant in Soho and indulged me in ten Martinis, which inspired me to go onto a further adventure to get some coke and find a rave to celebrate this great achievement. Somehow, I ended up in Hackney.

Sometime later after picking up the drugs; I started talking to these guys on the street. One guy was celebrating his fortieth birthday and guess what his name was…. Stephen! I was teasing him for living with his mum at his age and he seemed to grow fond of me. As my phone was almost out of charge, I decided to go with this Stephen guy, to his friend's flat to get it charged. A creepy surprise, the flat door was green and number 5a, just like my love Stephen's flat number and door.

The guy wanted me so much he pushed me down on the floor and tried to force himself on me. I could not believe what was happening. What happened when I was 16 was happening again, with a guy who had the same name as the love of my life and in the flat number identical to his.

It felt like some cosmic joke being played on me, but I knew that this was Bufo showing me what I was doing to myself. So, I had to fight the guy, I saw red, and I had to get out. The thought in my mind was to beat him up, get out from his hold and run, but it wasn't so easy, as he was a big man. After kicking, biting and punching I managed to get out, took my stuff and ran out of the flat screaming how he could have done that to me after I told him my story about me being abused at sixteen.

I did not know where I was, I was very high so the anxiety from drugs and what I just through was unbearable. All I could think about was I need more drugs, just need to get the fix, I cannot go on!

I was on the verge of a huge breakdown and I just could not bear it, so I needed to stop those feelings. Luckily, it was 11am, and my dealer was awake. It took me about forty minutes to pick up my stash from East London, then I travelled all the way to South London to a female friend who was always 'on it' and she was the perfect person to help me deal with what just happened. By deal with it I mean get high with me and talk to me about it. Let me vent. It was a bad idea, but I was a sucker for those.

Three days down the line, many grams of coke and loads of wine later, I was barely functioning. I got a taste of what it feels like to be a functioning drug addict. We met up with the friend's family and hung out with them as if we were sober. Hours later paranoia was kicking in and I tried very hard not to think of what just happened to me, and what I am doing to myself to get over it. This party had to end when we could not get any more drugs. I have decided to make my way home. I got a taxi to the shop to get strong, cheap alcohol. As I drank it, I was thinking how I cannot carry on this way; I either die or fix this mess I have become. I wondered what other situations I'll get myself into, what other danger I will have to go through to finally wake up.

I got home and managed to fall asleep after drinking about half a bottle of this horrible drink. The next day was hell, I was not able to comprehend how I did what I did and how I carried on thinking that drugs will be the answer to cope with the emotional trauma I have experienced. I felt so stupid, and it was on this day, the 5th June 2019 that I made the decision to fix myself, to stop re-enacting my pain and traumas by causing myself further damage. I was done with the martyr mentality that abandonment, rejection, shame and grief had done for me, I was done with this extreme punishment for losing Stephen.

However, I have so much to be grateful for because his death brought me the biggest awakening of my soul's existence. Twin Flames is a phenomenon of one soul being divided into two. They meet when each one is ready to find their true self. Each party mirrors the other's wounds back to one another in order to liberate their soul. Sometimes only physical death brings on a death of an ego, i.e., a death of conditioning. It is the most difficult soulmate union to go through on Earth. The lessons are extreme as you read above, but eventually it brings hope and light after so many lifetimes of darkness.

I remember the day I found out Stephen had died, I called my mum, and to my surprise she held space for my suffering in the best way she could. As you already know my mum has not been the warmest of mothers whilst I was growing up, so I did not expect this level of support, care and love from her. This tragic moment of my life has given life to the relationship with my mum that I have never really had. I asked mum about the incident when I was sixteen. Ten years later, she said she wished I asked earlier as she could not remember it, so even though I had less rage, I still felt dissatisfied as I saw it as an easy way out, to block out the pain that situation caused me. However, after Stephen's death, I was able to forgive. It put many things into perspective and how Stephen's magic was already being sprinkled on my relationship with my mum.

During the lockdown of 2020 I spent two weeks with my mum, honestly, I was dreading it. I could not imagine us getting along for fourteen days straight, but we did, and we had loads of fun. Mum has changed dramatically and still surprises me with the warmth and love she's got for me now and is able to express it much more freely. There is still much work to do in our relationship, but we are building a positive foundation. The healing I have done over these last three years since Stephen's passing has shown up in my relationship with mum. The healing we do affects seven generations before us and seven generations after us. I am proud to see that all the work I have done so far is right in front of my face, in my mum.

My sobriety has really been rewarded by the universe. I have been on a Vice documentary about psychedelics, and I was able to express my grief during the episode. It's been seen by more than two million people, and it seems like with every view the pain became more manageable because I was feeling seen and heard.

What followed was the opportunity to be at the Spiritual Festival called 'Om Fest'. It was my first ever event with my Energy Healing business 'Shakti Essence '. I had minimal support from my peers. No one came to support me, but it just proved to be more special. This event was the beginning of the journey of me being seen as a healer, not as a porn star or an escort.

Also, in 2020 Universe surprised me even more when I got an invitation to a 'Women Who Dare to Desire' event, and I got chosen during a raffle to be one of the speakers. I was a number six just as I felt I would be, as that is my life path number. It opened up a few connections and gave me more confidence. That being said I still hid; I still did not want to be fully seen. I was scared. Sex work shame on top of childhood shame led me into hiding for more than ten years. I rarely mentioned sex work and if I did, it was not in places such as the above event. The shame was still very present last year, and I am working on it continuously, it's not something that just goes away.

In this book I have come out of the closet. Thanks to the pandemic I was able to let go of that long, tedious, shameful, yet empowering, fun, inhibition free chapter of my life. Which has made me resilient enough to stand strong in adversity but at the same time super fragile to really step into my power and my purpose as a woman, healer and a writer.

The amount of healing I have done is quite astonishing and I am nowhere near done. The grief was coming in layers, it still hits me, but now I do not have the desire to reach for coke or alcohol.

These moments are now easier to recognize. It can come out of nowhere, and get triggered by prospective new guys, or other experiences with people. I chose the grief lesson and learned to manage it as the years go by. I only just learned to let the emotions flow through me without reaching for anything to numb me, be it food, or everything I was addicted to in the last year, because in 2020 on Stephen's birthday I still had a huge desire to get mashed up.

I've learned to listen to my body more and pay extra care to my wellbeing. I learned to ask for help when my addictions started niggling at me. The people around me held me and that connection with them, lessened my desire to harm myself. Healthy food, practicing yoga, and meditating is a huge part of my recovery.

Don't get me wrong, I am not perfect and fall off the self-care routines often, and it takes a while to get back on it. What I have learned is that kindness always wins in these situations. The process that helped me massively is NVC, 'non-Violent Communication' by Marshall Rosenberg. It is an approach to communication based on principles of nonviolence. It is a method to increase empathy and improve the quality of life. The teachings came to me in the first year of pandemic in May and since then I am able to know myself and my needs and feelings better and communicate it with myself and others. It has improved my relationships in so many ways.

I really had to have many AHA moments regarding Stephen's passing, because during these three years that he's been gone, the pain and the blame would still be present. I eventually realised the beauty his death brought to me and that it saved my life. Quite frankly I would have been dead one way or another, being with him, taking so many drugs or after he proposed to his ex.

A week before my 30th I went through the toughest grief episode when I had to really let go of the pain associated with his death, it crept in on me like a rainy night, unannounced. It felt really dark, I stayed in bed crying, unable to function. The pain of letting him go has really crippled me and the sorrow was felt deep within my bones. However, I realised how much I healed because I just wept, without suppressing my pain. As soon as I allowed myself to feel all the dark, suppressed emotional wounds, I elevated in consciousness, I experienced the bliss of the 5th Dimensional awareness a day before my 30th birthday. That was immense confirmation that all the healing I have been doing was worth it.

Healing inner child and father/mother wounds has brought me to the point where I do not hate my parents. It has been the pivotal work on my biological foundation that brought me the awareness to not blame them for my traumatic upbringing.

The book 'Home Coming: Reclaiming and Honouring Your Inner Child' by Michael Bradshaw was the introduction to my inner child healing, along with the 'Wounded Woman' by Linda Schierse Leonard. These were pivotal 'light bulb moments' reading for the healing the 'father wound' within. I know that I chose this path to be able to share my experiences with others so they can heal through it and find the strength and inspiration to make those steps towards liberation.

The healing that I recently integrated after so many years is that all these years, I have been so disconnected from myself that I have kept attracting people who rejected me as much as I rejected myself. This got triggered by a person I lived with, and during the uncomfortable interactions through applying NVC principles I learned this lesson. I struggled to accept myself whether it was my looks, my traumas or my career. I could not unconditionally accept myself. It is still a process, but I have overcome the huge hurdle of being in victimhood. Without blaming everyone else and taking the responsibility for my own karma and lessons I have chosen to learn.

I see healing as a full body experience. I have been guided to use different modalities of healings during the years. Astrology has been a huge part of my healing and getting to know myself and understanding my relationship with others. I can proudly say this is my favourite and healthiest addiction.

Energy healing modalities that I am qualified in such as Usui and Karuna Reiki, Light of Lemuria, Universal Field and Munai Kay.

Other methods of healing such as meditations, healing circles, journaling and talking therapy including NVC. Body work- sacred colonic irrigations, juicing, water fasting, Transpersonal Pilates, yoga, Bowen technique, scanners, breathwork and Ayurveda to name a few.

The most significant healing which opened me up to be a responsible participant in my healing process was sacred medicine ceremonies. The experience I have gained through these modalities showed me that a full body approach works best. In this case the entire system with all bodies aligns with each other. Mental body cannot work well without the emotional body, and the physical body cannot coexist in balance if the rest of the bodies are out of sync.

After so many years trying to protect myself by numbing myself to not feel during my porn and escorting career, feeling so much was so overwhelming, and as I described it earlier in the chapter sometimes it was unbearable, I did not have the emotional resilience to cope with it. So, I really do understand how it feels like to be in that place but also, I am getting comfortable allowing myself to really feel the beauty of emotion. The depth of the emotion you can go into to deeply heal the wounds that have been present your entire life. The healing takes place in the entirety of the being. Within all the bodies, to reach the bliss that we all have free will to achieve.

My mission as a Sagittarius Sun with Aquarius Rising is to bring people onto their Ascension path and their authentic Truth. I am achieving that by bringing the authenticity of my path and the depth of the healing I have done so far, to be an emotionally sovereign, divine being. In Shakti Essence I began my career by working with inner child wounds, and as you have probably gathered the abandonment, the wound has been pretty huge in my lifetime and I am still healing it, but because of it I am able to help others.

Past life healing fascinates me, and I welcomed it into the healing sessions for further healing and clarity. The way my energy is right now it is quite hard to see that I have had and still do sometimes, self-esteem issues. I seem so vibrant and confident but that has taken a lot of work to build a strong foundation and what really helped me is immersing myself into sacred sexuality healing via Tantric massage and then studying Tantra. It reconnected me to my Inner Goddess that was laying doormat. The knowledge and the feelings of love for myself, learning Tantra turned into a body positivity journey as the more I heal the more I enjoy my body, it has gotten soft and lovely as I am getting older. I am enjoying the feminine aspect to this softness which makes me feel very sexy and Goddess-like. I am driven to inspire women to find that same beauty in their natural silhouette, whatever shape we are in the present moment.

On the 5th June 2021 it was the second anniversary of me being sober and clean. I finally feel like I am getting my biggest recognition from the Universe as I have always wanted to write a book. Back in Lithuania my literature teacher in high school was quite strict with me because she saw great potential in me as a writer and storyteller. Here I am today, sixteen years later, taking part in this anthology and it has taken so many twists and turns, traumas and sufferings, emotional maturity, transparency and vulnerability to be able to bring my story out into the world.

To illuminate the path into healing for so many people who struggle with suicidal thoughts hourly and the immense pressure of life responsibilities doubled up with the traumas from childhood. The imprints of the traumas from the past lives can keep us stuck in repeating patterns for lifetimes. For me, this lifetime feels like a lifetime, where against all the odds I am removing the shackles of my ancestral karma.

The present moment brings me to summarize all the experiences I have gained over the years in the sex industry. An authentic, clear perspective of what I have seen and experienced. I am passionate to show people that our wounding does not have to lead us into the glamorized sex work. Most people think it's an easy way to make money, but it's far from it.

I want to educate the Youth about the reality of the industry and what it really entails. I hope to inspire them to seek a different way to earn money and to understand why they feel drawn to seek out this career. My approach to is to bring consciousness and truth into the adult work and sex itself. Shakti Essence's mission is to guide sex workers who want to retire but do not know how to do it and to show women the way to liberate their dormant feminine essence and empower them to embrace their wild side.

Writing this chapter has been such a cathartic experience for me and I hope it will be the same for you. I hope it brings you inspiration and strength to carry on and find the most suitable ways to heal, even the decades of the darkest times will eventually see the light. As you heal, the light will shine brighter and brighter and your smile will get wider and wider.

REFLECTIONS

REFLECTIONS

Erica Lopez

Erica Lopez is an English high school teacher who has taught for twenty-four years. She is dedicated to empowering her students.

She is a speaker, author, and life coach, and her goal is to help others find love within themselves. She has a YouTube channel called Vida Loca coaches. She feels teens and kids need to be understood, and she dedicates her work to teach students that they need to reframe their struggles.

As a psychic/medium she helps people connect with their loved ones. She is an energy healer, and a chakra specialist. She helps people connect to their higher self, and she can be found at **ericalifecoaching.com**

Overcoming the Lowest Moment in my Life

BY ERICA LOPEZ
US

When I attended college, I was given the task to read Milton's *Doctrine of Discipline and Divorce*. I became immediately intrigued by his message, which was so ahead of its time. He wrote this doctrine to the state and the church claiming that people should be allowed to divorce. Regarding religion, Milton claimed that people would sin more if they stayed unhappily married. Regarding the state, why should people stay married if they were miserable and the state had no jurisdiction in marriage. Growing up, being raised Catholic, I attributed my divorce to failure. I did not want to leave my marriage, I had low self-worth, and I held onto a dead marriage for dear life. In my perspective, I loved him. I was so attached that I had no idea where I started and where he began. I became tied to his emotions and behaviours, taking responsibility for everything. I blamed myself.

When you hear something over and over, you begin to believe it. That is exactly what happened to me. I took the blame and shame because I heard those words over and over. He said everything was my fault, and because of my blurred attachment, I believed it was true. The breakdown of my marriage was my fault, the failures of my kids were my fault, his misery was my fault, everything was my fault. Was I dysfunctional? Yes,

I was incredibly dysfunctional. And the worst part was that I hated myself, and only lived to accommodate him. It was awful. We married in 1999 and had the tumultuous journey of ups and downs for the next sixteen years.

I had been asked many times why I chose to stay for so long. The only thing I can say is that you learn when you learn. Once, I went on my first and only date, when this man said to me,

"You are a slow learner."

I asked, *"Why do you say that?"*

He replied, *"Because you know if it is going to work out with someone within five years and it took you fifteen."*

I kept quiet because I knew he was right. I never saw him again, but he told me exactly what I needed to hear. I learned to not waste my time trying to fix something that cannot be fixed. If it does not work with my person within five years, then I must conclude to move on. I chose to stay because I associated divorce with failure. Similar to the mistake that Gatsby makes in *The Great Gatsby*, I also included someone in my dream that did not want to be in it. In *The Great Gatsby,* Daisy had her own life and vision that sadly, did not include Gatsby. She would have an affair with him, but nothing further than that. I wanted my husband and my two kids to be a happy family, living together until old age. Not because I was content or he was kind to me, but because I did not want my children to be without their father; I could not handle another death. When a relationship ends, it's similar to a death. At this point, both my parents and close family members had died, and I did not want to feel abandoned by another end. I could not make him love me or force him to be with me. My ex no longer wanted to be married. He wanted the freedom to live his life, and not be scrutinized by my self-righteous behaviour. I feared I wasn't good enough that he was going to leave me, and cheat on me again. Fear was bigger in my head than it was in real life because my worst nightmare had come true.

I do not want to villainize my ex-husband. He lived a difficult childhood. When he was a child no one rescued him from the dysfunction. He became insecure and felt he could not be enough for me, so he looked for women to rescue. He tried to save someone that would make him proud of being there for someone who needed him but did this at the expense of my children and me. During reconciliation we really tried, we went to a Retrouvaille Retreat, and participated in the Marriage Encounter journey. We even got trained to teach others how to heal their marriage through these organizations. However, the woman he cheated on me with was deeply rooted in his heart. She was a family friend. Her son would often play with my son, and the kids and I both trusted her. My ex-husband and the other woman built a closeness before the affair even started. Her husband left her, and my ex-husband began the affair three months after her husband left. The affair continued for nine months before I found out. It was a very difficult trauma of betrayal to deal with, but it was a part of my life that needed to happen. Eventually, it allowed me to clear the muck from the deep trauma I carried, and slowly let me heal. We tried our best, but he psychologically could not let her go, and we lived with a ghost in our home.

Our dysfunction was too deep and our patterns too strong for us to break the cycle. We utilized what we had learned to try and succeed in the marriage, but he carried the guilt of abandoning her, and could not forgive himself for that. For several years, we lived on this crazy roller coaster trying to fix the unmendable. I could not understand why he did not love me. *What was wrong with me?* I was the mother of his children, but still, he loved her and only *cared* about me. He stayed for our kids, not because he wanted things to work out. He was afraid of them hating him and knew the milestones that were coming in their life. Our son was going through middle school, then high school and he did not want to miss those moments. Those moments where he wanted to cheer his son on through his baseball season or take his daughter to her father-daughter dance. He chose to stay when deep down in his heart, he did not want to. He wanted to see if the other woman was his forever love and staying with me robbed him of that opportunity. He continued to stay with us when his heart was somewhere else, and her ghostly presence continued to haunt our lives.

His love for her was so great, that I started picking up destructive patterns. I began binge drinking and putting my children through the craziness of my alcoholism. The funny thing is, I never had a drinking problem, but when you undergo so much emotional and traumatic pain, you just want the pain to end. I was extremely high functioning. I always went to work and was responsible. And this is why I mainly binge drank on the weekends. I would drink, listen to music, and cry endlessly. I did not see how my behaviour was hurting my children. I did not see how I was not present which forced them to care for each other. As parents, we never realise just how much we can damage our kids. We only see things from our perspective and cannot comprehend what it is like to perceive what our children experience. I became aware of the damage I caused my kids when I first corrected my son's grammar on one of his college papers. Being a sociology major, he was enrolled in a class about marriage. He had written, "My mother was so wrapped up in the dysfunction of my father, and thus, my sister and I were neglected." Blinded, I viewed myself as a good mother, but his writing elucidated that feeding, clothing, and providing for children is simply inadequate. I parented physically, but both my ex and I did not parent, emotionally. Assigned to write about the most traumatic experience of his life, he chose to write about my suicide attempt. "I cannot believe that my mother would choose to try to die and leave me here with my alcoholic father." These words *stung*. It opened a portal to the dark place I remained in, that I yearned for the pain to end, oblivious to the trauma I caused my children. I believed I no longer served a purpose for them, and if I died, then they would not have to worry about their alcoholic mother. I developed an alcohol problem to deal with the pain of my ex's constant infidelity. Still, unwilling to leave him.

Alcoholism is a draining disease that plagued both my ex and me.

One of the 'gifts' my ex-husband left was my deep intuition. He was a serial cheater, and I learned that if my gut was 'screaming', then he was cheating. The sad part is that he would constantly gaslight me. I believed I was crazy because once again; when you hear something repeatedly, you begin to believe it. This is the danger of manipulation and gaslighting, you start to lose trust in yourself. Already deeply insecure, now I could not trust my instinct. I learned from this point forward, no matter how crazy someone says I am, my instinct is always right. I recall one summer when I knew my ex-husband was cheating. I couldn't figure out *how* because he would go to work, then come straight home, so there was no time. Nothing made sense. I could not understand who, or when, this was happening. My ex used the fact that he was never out, and at work, so to him in my sick mind, I thought he was cheating. I had no answer. I did not know. All I knew was the voice in my gut was screaming. Years later, I found out that he was having an affair during his lunch hour. He worked in sales, always travelling to companies to sell staffing services provided by the company he worked for. In one of his outings, he met someone, and they would meet during his lunchtime at hotels. When I found this out years after we had ended our marriage, I was relieved because I was not crazy and right the entire time. This taught me that trust is internal, and our instinct is always right. I know I was dysfunctional for trying to control a man who could not be faithful and losing myself in the process. I lost my identity, and my whole life revolved around him which is no way to live.

My ex and I tried to heal our marriage before I left the house, and I rented my apartment for me and my children. We tried to help others heal their marriages as well, by giving classes and telling couples our story. The only problem was we did not seek individual help to deal with the residue of emotions that were left from his betrayal. I could not understand *how he could care for someone who caused me and the kids so much pain*. I was emotionally immature and did not realise that he was just as guilty. He was the one that was married, more importantly, the one who pursued another relationship outside of our marriage. It was easy to villainize her, but that rage blinded me from believing that they had a real relationship. I could not accept that. Had I gotten individual help, maybe I could have seen the reality of his relationship and let that possibly lead me to the point of accepting that my husband loved someone else. If he had gotten individual help, maybe he would have learned from a neutral perspective that he made a mistake and needed to reach the point of accepting and forgiving himself. Maybe he could have learned the tools to let her go, and maybe he could've used them to work on the areas that kept us apart. When people want to survive infidelity, they need to do everything they can to heal individually, and then heal their relationship. We worked so much on the relationship that we ignored our own healing, which led us to the point of despair and misery.

I went insane. It was hard to trust him. He lied and cheated so many times. I did not know what the truth was and what wasn't. I had little faith in myself living in a video game, awaiting the next obstacle or challenge that was coming my way. Was I going to walk on eggshells today? Were my kids going to anger him today? Was I going to feel in my gut instinct that he was cheating today? Is he going to explode while drinking today? Or was I going to enjoy the pleasure of a loving peaceful home? I had no idea. During this time, my life was in survival mode. My emotions were so tied to him. To what he said, how he acted, and I had no sense of self. I lived for him and had no room for anything else. No wonder, my son and daughter felt neglected. What I learned about trust is that trust is not about trusting the other person, trust is really about trusting yourself, then trusting God. The reason women with low self-esteem struggle with trust is because they do not trust themselves. That is the issue of issues. When I did not trust myself, I would calculate every decision, and I was afraid of the outcome. More so, I lived in perpetual fear, and I lived with constant anxiety. After having a rough childhood, I realised one of the most familiar feelings I had was fear. Fear became comfortable for me, and I took it into adulthood. I must trust myself. If I trust myself, I'll have faith that I will do what is best for me when confronted with unacceptable behaviour. This led to me learning how to adult my inner child. When my inner child is throwing tantrums, I must advocate and stand up for her, say '*I am an adult, I am here, and I will protect you.*' My inner child must trust me, and that only happens when I trust myself.

In my insanity, I put a device in his phone where I could read all his text messages, see his photos, and read all his emails. I had access to his email previously, but eventually, I told him. He changed the password. I was a professional stalker. It was pretty sad and pathetic, but that is all I had to see if he was lying. Since he was so incapable of telling me the truth. It was unhealthy for me and made me emotionally ill. The app also recorded his conversations, and I noticed that he was receiving calls from an unavailable number. I instantly knew it was her. When this happened, I confronted him, which he immediately denied. I had to find the recording from all the files from the program, and I played it for him. Giving him no choice, but to admit what he was doing. I had it. I confronted the other woman at her work, and that was a mistake. It played differently in my head. I should have told her if you want him, then you could have him. But I said, "you are hurting my children, so stay away from my husband." She said, "he looks for me." I said," you know right from wrong, and you're breaking up my family." She did not care. My ex-husband was mad because I confronted her. We could not talk. I was irrational and out of control. I think that night I told him to lock his bedroom door because I would have killed him.

I went to an Alcoholics Anonymous meeting because I was newly sober and just finished an outpatient rehab program. After about four months sober, I had this thorn on my side that kept pricking me after I thought I already pulled it out. He was talking to the woman he loved again after all the work we did. All the retreats, all the classes, all the therapy, and he was back to talking to her. We were so far gone from each other that there was no point of no return, but I did not want to lose the life I knew because it was familiar. I grew up in childhood with so much chaos, so this was normal. I became afraid of the unknown. I found out on a Monday morning that he was talking to her again, and I decided to kick him out on Friday. What I did not realise was that him leaving would trigger my childhood abandonment. It would take me back to being that little girl whose mother just died and was now battling this world alone. I had no idea that I would feel so useless and so foolish for loving him. So much so, it took me down a spiral of destruction and pain. He left and met up with her that night. I called and called until he turned his phone off. He moved to his sister's house. He blocked me and had nothing to say to me. I could not handle that rejection from him, and I did not want the kids to see me in that awful state. I chose to leave my kids at his sister's house and went to buy alcohol to get drunk by myself. I did not care about my sobriety, and all I wanted was the pain to end. I called my siblings while sobbing endlessly. The more I drank, the sadder I got. I listened to music that resonated with the pain I was feeling. I kept crying and crying. I was alone, drinking by myself, and hoping to cry it all out.

SUICIDE ATTEMPT

Fate had different plans, and it did not work out the way I wanted it to. I figured I would wake up the next morning, dust myself off, and go on living. Never in a million years, did I think that the events that transpired that night would happen, but they did. Abandonment is a dreadful trauma that can throw an educated adult woman into a spiral of irrational behaviour. I was left, and I was left for someone else. Every insecurity formed from childhood rose to the surface. I felt worthless; I was not good enough; there was something wrong with me. Everyone who bullied me growing up were suddenly right; I was a failure. I could not get this man to love me, and my marriage ended in divorce. The problem with going down the rabbit hole is that once you begin to spiral, you cannot stop. You go down deeper and deeper. My biggest mistake in all of this was that I made him my everything. I put all my good qualities: my love, my self-esteem, my caring heart, my hard work, my independence, and gave it all in a basket, just for him to drop it. I had no idea that the basket belonged to me and that *I* needed to care for it, not anybody else. I felt so alone, depressed, hurt, but I wanted to get through it myself. If you are ever in this state, ask for help, never try and do it alone. Countless people can be there for you. What we need to do is just to reach out and ask for help. I felt so much shame and embarrassment for my moment of weakness. I broke once again after four months of sobriety. I did not ask for help, and as a result, I tried to take my life.

I was alone in my room, my ex was calling me, and I was already drunk. In my right mind, I would not have answered, but I was drunk and who makes good choices when they are drunk. We argued and fought. He was angry that I was drunk, so I hung up and threw my phone against the wall, causing it to break. I guess that concerned my children and ex-husband, and they made the mistake of coming to the house. I swear to you, I had no intention of taking my life. In those moments, it was not even a thought of mine.

At first, when he got there, I was angry. Why could they not leave me alone? I was not breaking the law. I was an adult woman drinking away her sorrows or trying to anyway. The fact that he brought my daughter was the worst thing because I had already put her through so much with my alcoholic drama. I did not need her saying I was a bad mother and reminding me of what an awful person I was for not being able to stay sober, nor how I was such a big disappointment to her. She pointed her finger towards me, and asked, "Why Mum, why?" Again, I was angry because he chose not to leave me alone, and he brought my daughter, so she could see me in my low state. He blocked me for a full twenty-four hours, and did not want to take my calls or read my texts, so why did he have to come while I was in my lowest state? It was not his fault. I chose to get drunk; I chose to go down that rabbit hole, but him bringing my daughter and leaving me again in my low state did not help. In the commotion, my daughter left her cell phone and they left. Right before he left; however, he came back right as he was leaving and looked at me with such disdain and disgust, as if I was a piece of trash, *and that look I could not handle.* When he left, I said, "Please don't leave me," and then he gave me the look again and left.

I grabbed my daughter's phone, and simply texted "Take care of the kids." I was crying uncontrollably. I was a terrible mother. How could I hurt my kids so much? I was a piece of trash to him. I no longer mattered. What was the point of being in so much pain, to keep on breathing? I had let everyone down. I broke my sobriety. I could not stay sober. I could not be there for my children, and he did not love me. Why would I even bother to continue living? I was a failure, a nobody, and I could no longer deal with the pain. I had a beer in my hand and from the corner of my eye, I saw his Advil PM pills. I did not stop to think. It was an irrational decision. I just grabbed whatever was in the bottle and swallowed them. I did not think twice. I did not call anyone. I wanted to numb myself to death. Eventually, I fell into a deep sleep. I do not remember exactly what happened, but from what I was told, my sister-in-law and brother-in-law came over. My daughter had to come through the window. I had locked the entire house because I did not want anyone else to bother me. My sister-in-law called 911, the ambulance came, and I woke up in the hospital. My sister-in-law stayed with me. She was upset and disappointed, but I was grateful that she did not lecture me. She stayed until three in the morning and left. I had to drink a black liquid that was supposed to help dissolve and encapsulate the pills. I was blessed to not have my stomach pumped. My vitals were fine, so they let me stay in the hospital until they transferred me into a mental institution. He never visited me in the hospital. Still, I was not ready to let him go. I feared the unknown. My life was not happy, and I lived in a mentally abusive household, but I knew that life; I did not know what it would be like to live alone, and that fear engulfed me.

My doctor was angry at me. He acted very cold and callous. His energy was like, "I do not have time for this." He only entered my room once. He checked and looked at my chart, then the next two times he simply stood by the door. I was not sure if he was frustrated with me because I tried to die, or maybe I triggered a memory in him, but I reminded him of someone he knew. I tried to manipulate my way out of there. I claimed I was trying to get high, so I only took a couple to improve my drunkenness. They had not told the hospital staff that my husband was leaving me, so they were under the impression I had some form of support. I did not want to miss work, so I begged my social worker to let me go home, but the doctor would not sign. The second time he came in, he warned the staff, "No, she is a 51/50." He looked at me, and said, "We are not sending you home. For what? So, you can try and kill yourself again?" and he walked out. I stayed in the hospital until about 2 pm on Sunday. My husband never came. I was sad because I thought he would at least stop by, but he didn't. I had to be transferred to a mental institution in Torrance, California. An ambulance picked me up and admitted me.

This was not my first time being in a mental institution. In 2003, my father died of cirrhosis of the liver, and my thirty-three-year-old cousin died two weeks later of a heart attack. I then fell into a deep depression. My therapist at the time suggested I go to the hospital. I did. I felt so empty, numb, and sad. I went to the mental institution, where they kept me for five days. My ex-husband had to fight to get me out. I knew not to take the medication because that was the excuse, they used to keep me longer. I knew to eat all my food, go to all the group meetings, keep myself busy, and emotionally healthy while I was there. I wanted to do everything I could to get out of the mental institution.

The thing that struck me the most about the whole experience was that I was not the only one there who tried to die over a guy. There was a nurse who took pills, an executive secretary who cut herself, and me. It made me realise that so many beautiful, strong women were so attached to men who did not love them, and that included me. I wanted to get out of the hospital as soon as possible. I did not belong there, but I had to come face to face with my alcoholism. In retrospect. I realised if I had not been drinking, I would not have taken the pills. I needed to stop drinking, and I had to heal and try and keep my family together.

My sister drove eight hours from Tucson to come to see me. I started going to Alcoholics Anonymous meetings and tried to be sober. My ex-husband wanted me to go to a sober living home where recovering alcoholics can live with a low rental fee, but with very strict rules. The rules included a minimum number of meetings, a curfew, a sponsor, and how we must follow house rules. I refused. I had deeply hurt my children, and I needed to make amends. I was so grateful I did not die, and although I had to do so much work to try and heal; at least, I had a chance to recover and heal with my children. I had to take their anger and hurt, but I knew if I consistently showed them how sorry I was and how much I was working to change, then they could, one day, find it in their hearts to forgive me. My sister tried to stay close, but it was too painful for her. I became a burden and brought her down with me. She could not handle my choices, and the pain I was experiencing. She loved me, but she needed to save herself. I worked hard with the kids, and I lived in gratitude for a month. I knew my ex-husband was still seeing the other woman, so I asked him to stay in the house for thirty days, then he could leave. I was going to several twelve-step meetings regularly, so I knew I would be able to stand on my own. I let him be. For the first time, my goal was me, and I needed to stay alive for these kids.

After thirty days, he chose not to leave. He stopped speaking to the other woman, but it did not matter because we had an ever-present ghost in our home. He loved her, and I had to stand by and witness him crying for her. He would play sad music, drink, then cry and cry for his long-lost love. What I realised later, was that when you focus on what you have lost, then you miss out on what you have. He struggled so much to let her go, carrying so much guilt that even though he stopped talking to her, she lived in his heart and memory. We were now in survival mode. I had that tracking device on his phone, and I could see all his messages and hear all his phone calls. It was making me sick, so as much as I tried in this marriage, there was no way it was going to work. I became obsessed, wanting to know his every move, and that is no way to live. My turning point was I found out that my ex was bringing his lover to his sister's house, so they all could meet her. We were still living in the same home, and she was being accepted as part of his family. At that point, I knew it was time to go.

I decided to give the thirty-day notice for the house and started searching for an apartment for my children and me. He was upset because I was leaving, but he left me no other choice. I could no longer stay in this relationship. I was losing control. There was one day that I wanted to kill him. While I was working, my brother-in-law called me and said the dog got out of the gate. I called my ex-husband, and he was with her, and I heard her voice in the background. I told him to go and get the dog, he did and put the dog back in the backyard. At work, I was fuming, but I could always function regardless of my emotions. I left work, and I wanted to literally kill him. My thoughts were racing, and I was picturing stabbing him with a knife, but as I was driving home, I remembered a story I read in Melody Beatie's book, *Co-dependent No More*; a beautiful model wife was chasing her husband around the house with a knife in front of the children because she was tired of his cheating. For one second, I reflected and said "No, that is not me." People go to jail for what they do, and not for what they think. I calmed down, and I ended up going to a church. At the church, I had the conviction that I was not alone. I met up with my friend, went to dinner, and talked and I did not go home until 9:00 pm. At that point, I calmed down enough to face him and realised that this too would eventually pass.

I moved out into my apartment, and we were apart for five months. Then once again, there we were trying to work things out, and he moved back in again. This time was different because it was my apartment, and I could set my boundaries. I told him that if he wanted to get drunk and miss her, he could do that at a bar and not at my apartment. Then in January, he left again and went back to her. That was when I decided to work hard to try and let go.

There is an art to letting go. Almost like trying to hold onto a butterfly, but if you do not let it go, it will die. I was so addicted to this man, but I knew that I had no other choice. I had to get off that roller coaster ride, so I can have my chance to find happiness. It was easy to blame him, but in reality, it was not his fault. I was allowing him and his energy into my life. My biggest wake-up call was when I started dating. The first person that I had a fling with was a replica of my ex-husband. This guy ghosted me and disappeared, and that was the biggest gift he could give me because that is when I committed to working on my healing. The problem with perpetual relationships is that a woman dates the same person repeatedly, but in a different body, and the danger in that is that it hurts children. I did not want to put my children around another man who was going to make them walk on eggshells. At that point, I worked on inner child healing, and I started learning about how men are and how they think. I could now date with strategy and a game plan. I wrote down the ten qualities I wanted in a man and dated men that I would never previously date. One of the key things I looked for was a man who was a good father, and I found him.

I met an amazing man that was a single father in the middle of a divorce. I was in the same situation. I was not yet divorced, but we learned to value each other. We treated each other well, and he is an amazing father. At age forty-two, I manifested my son, and we had him on November 7, 2016. Our romantic relationship has had ups and downs, and a couple of breakups, but we have managed to heal and meet each other's needs. What I learned was if you just let go, you will not know what beautiful life you could have. I have a beautiful family today: my stepson, who just graduated and is attending college next year; my stepdaughter, who is only 13; my adult special needs daughter, who is twenty-one; my four-year-old son; my oldest son, his wife, and my granddaughter. I would never have all these beautiful beings in my life had I not let go. I am beyond grateful that I moved from the dark space in my life and that I can help others through my teaching, coaching, speaking, and now my writing.

INNER CHILD HEALING

One of the big things I realised in my healing journey was how much I neglected my inner child. I was neglected growing up, so I had no idea that I had to hear, fight for, advocate, and love my inner child. In moments of injustice, my inner child would tantrum, and I as an adult would lose control and be angry and irrational. I realised that I did not trust myself, and my decisions because I did not know how to set boundaries, or how to advocate for myself. I took workshops on healing my inner child, and I learned a technique to carry around a baby picture of myself and to love myself like I would that child. It became my responsibility to protect her, care for her, and love her. As a child, I was raised to not have a voice and to put up with unacceptable behaviour, and there were no adults to advocate for me, so I carried this inner child trauma. In times of crisis, my inner child would lead me to make bad choices, or act irrationally. I learned to write letters to my inner child telling her how much I love her and to forgive me for my mistakes. I built a relationship with my little girl, and she knows that today she is valued, and she matters. I learned to adult my inner child. When she was angry, she would throw tantrums because she did not get her way, I would calm her down by saying I am here, I will protect you, you are okay. You may not have been loved and protected as a child, but today as an adult you can love, protect, advocate, support and believe in your inner child.

TWELVE STEPS PROGRAMS

I started Al-Anon in December of 2006, and it aided me in many ways regarding my childhood and current situation. Al-Anon is a program that helps families who have been affected by a person's drinking. I grew up with my alcoholic father, and I learned so many unhealthy coping mechanisms that I had to unlearn. I was obsessive, controlling, manipulative, a victim, self-righteous, and a martyr. I never realised that I had choices and that I could be happy despite my circumstances. I entered Alanon due to my ex-husband's alcoholism. His behaviour was affecting me, and I blamed him for my miserable life. My children were getting help as well, in Pre-Alateen and Alateen. I think exposing my children to the program was one of the best decisions I made. I started looking at my own erratic and irrational behaviour. I started noticing my character defects and realizing that I was responsible for a lot of the dysfunction in my home. For four years I was a dedicated member of the program and learned so many tools and techniques to live life effectively. I learned slogans like *'easy does it,' 'this too shall pass,' 'what is the next indicated step,' 'one day at a time,'* and *'let go and let God.'* When my brain switched to crisis mode, these slogans helped me come back to reality. I also had an extraordinarily gentle sponsor who taught me how to say, *"I love you."* A sponsor is a person who guides you through the twelve steps, and who supports you in times of struggle. When I came into the program, saying 'I love you' was still uncomfortable and foreign to me. I would say it to my young children, but not to my siblings or anyone else for that matter. When my sponsor would hang up the phone, she would say 'I love you,' and I would feel so clammy and weird about it, but luckily, now I am comfortable with saying 'I love you.'

In 2010, I shifted from Al-Anon to Sanon. Sanon is a twelve-step program that helps families who have been affected by someone's sexaholic. This program was significantly more difficult for me. It brought up that my first sexaholics were the perpetrators who molested me as a child. My father had to work a lot, so I would be abused by my babysitter's teenage boys. That specific part of my life was very difficult for me to deal with. During this time, I began suffering from anxiety and lost my sense of direction. On one occasion, I left my sponsor's home, and drove 20 miles away from my home, struggling to find my way back. That occurred several times. I was triggered and had a memory that was too overwhelming, that I became like a child, lost in the store, trying to find her parents. This is when I also began working on my inner child. I could, for the most part, handle my depression, but the anxiety was especially difficult because I could not make sense of what was happening to my body and mind. I learned to meditate and breathe and calm myself down. Sanon taught me that it was not my fault and that my ex-husband's cheating had nothing to do with me. They taught me about my behaviour, and how snooping and looking through his things is just as bad as counting the drinks he was having. It taught me that

I had to trust God and that I could trust God when I could not trust myself. Through this program, I was able to raise my self-esteem and love myself in a way I never thought possible. The reason Twelve- Step programs are so healing is that you realise you are not alone, and others truly understand what it is like to be you. Sanon helped me be grateful, and I also built long-lasting friendships with an incredible bond because we know each other's pain, but we also know each other´s experience, strength, and hope.

Alcoholics Anonymous came after because my drinking problem began at age 35, and although it lasted three years, I had a foundation in Twelve steps because of my previous programs. Alcoholics Anonymous helps people stay sober and teaches them the tools to live a serene life. The hardest part of Twelve step programs is keeping yourself in a state of peace and serenity. Alcoholics Anonymous helps me stay sober even to this day, and it reminds me to take one day at a time. I stopped drinking on 12th April 2014, and I have never looked back. I did not like who I was and how I became when I drank. I am most proud to say that my step kids have never seen me take a drink and my toddler has never seen me drunk. I have done a lot of healing with my older kids and made amends with them. I know I am deeply responsible for the pain they experienced due to my drinking, but I have committed to being the best mother I can be for them. Shame and guilt do not serve anyone, and beating myself over past mistakes hurts me, so I must stand in my power and own my mistakes because that is the only way to change and learn to be different and grow. I constantly recite the mantra that says, "I completely love and accept myself." I say it over and over because I know I can punish myself psychologically for the things I cannot change, which includes my past. Today I can recognize my need for a meeting or when I need to leave an environment that I am not comfortable in. I have learned that I am the most important person in my life, and to say no when I mean no. I learned to be in tune with my emotions and my desire to numb, and I remember my suicide attempt and it gets my head straight real fast, and I make a call or go to a meeting.

COACHING AND THERAPY

For therapy, you must choose the right therapist. My ex-husband and I went to therapy for a year, and it was a waste of time. We were angry every time we left, and there were no solutions or skills that we learned. I went to individual therapy, and it helped some, but I learned more from the twelve steps and hiring my coach. When I hired my coach, it particularly impacted me. When I first started working with my coach, I was deeply insecure and felt unworthy of myself. I had no idea what I needed and expected in a relationship. My boyfriend and I had broken up in April of 2017, and now in September of that same year, we were working on getting back together. We had a son who was born in November of 2016, and I was not sure about getting back together. He had hurt me, and I felt that we did not want the same things. I wanted a fully committed relationship where we could live together and raise our son, but he did not agree. We started sharing custody with my son, and it was the hardest thing I had to do because my son was only five months old. I was with my children 24/7, and now my infant son was living in two homes, but I stood my ground and refused to get back together unless we were to commit to moving in together. My coach taught me that I was the prize, that I needed to show up for myself and fill my cup. She taught me my value, and I had to work on seeing myself through her eyes. I was stubborn and I did not listen, so she once told me if I refuse to do what she advised, I would have to find someone else for my coach. That was a wake-up call for me because she taught me that I was over-giving. I had purchased concert tickets, ballet tickets, steak dinners, and she said you cannot take your boyfriend. I was shocked. I knew that if I did not listen, she would fire me as her client. It was hard, but I listened, and it opened a world to me that I didn't know existed. She said I was over giving in the relationship, and that I needed to give to myself and others who loved me. When you overcompensate, over accommodate, or over give the person you are with may take you for granted and not value you.

She always reminded me that I had choices, that nothing was a life sentence. She also taught me that you never stay for children. Those children would rather come from a broken home than be in one and suffer through the dysfunction of their parents. She taught me to believe in myself and inspired me to speak, write, and get out of my comfort zone. Due to her lessons, I have been able to publicly speak on Global Virtual Panels about domestic violence, sexual assault, depression, anxiety, and infidelity. She encouraged me to enter a speaking competition and now I am in their program. The biggest lesson she taught me was that this work of helping others is too important not to follow through with it.

PERSONAL GROWTH

Today, I am just looking to constantly personally grow. I know many people say they do not have the finances to help themselves, but there is no excuse. There is so much out there that can help you heal. There are no dues or fees for Twelve-step programs, and if you can, donate to group expenses. Another thing that can help is to follow people that inspire you. My personal favourites are Dave Hollis, Trent Shelton, Mel Robbins, Brendon Burchard, Gloria Atanmo, Anthony Trucks, and Jamie Kern Lima. One of the best investments I have made this year was Growth Day. It includes many of these speakers sharing a story every month on a specific topic. You cannot raise your consciousness unless you learn from those who have done so already. I am talking about finding peace and acceptance in your life, and these people have worked every single day to hold on to their peace of mind. Another resource is YouTube. There are so many meditations that can help you calm your mind. Yoga heals trauma, which can help your body heal from your past trauma. Gabby Bernstein has her *All is Well Meditation* on her YouTube channel. It's only five minutes, but it will put you in the right mindset. The only way to overcome your past and live your best future is to do the work. Nothing will change, unless you put in the work to change, and download a new positive program in your brain. Another thing is to watch your self-talk.

It is not acceptable for you to treat yourself badly or put yourself down. You have to overcome it with a positive thought that you say out loud ten times. If you say to yourself, "I am dumb," you have to say "I am smart, "ten times to overpower that one negative thought.

INVESTING IN YOURSELF TO HEAL

Since then, I have hired several coaches to help me clear my blocks, paid for many courses, and participated in different programs to help me raise my consciousness. The one thing I can say that I have learned from everything is that we bring the energy that we fear into our lives. For example, I was being interviewed at 4 in the morning because I needed to do it in a quiet space. I told my fiancé to stay quiet. That, right there, was my mistake. I should have had the intention that everything was going to flow smoothly, but I feared that he would make noise, and guess what, he did. Consider the energy you are bringing into the situation; you are attracting what you do not want at times. I discovered that as human beings, we all have fears and anxiety at one point. The difference between leaders and people who are successful compared to us is that they know how to manage their emotions better and connect to their higher-self more often. The answers are out there. You can make it your life's work to heal. Healing will give you the ability to change your family dynamic, the people around you, and break the cycle of dysfunction in future generations of your lineage.

You may have suffered in your life tremendously, but your past no longer has to be your future. You must get used to saying the word 'No' and mean it. You must put yourself first and love yourself. Love is meant to be overflowing from your cup, and you cannot pour from an empty cup. We tend to give and give, often leaving nothing for ourselves, and therein lies the dilemma. It is like when you are on a plane with a child. When the oxygen mask falls, you must put it on yourself first, and then the child. As parents we make the mistake of giving it all to our kids, and we are barely surviving. Try giving all that love to yourself and see what a better parent you will be. Consider doing this exercise, make a list of all your exes. If there are too many, then consider your long-term relationships, and then realise that the one thing they all had in common was you. Look at their similarities and differences and consider if any were dysfunctional. Then ask yourself the question, *"What inside you felt the need to attract this person in your life?"* Most of the time, you are repeating a childhood pattern. If you are, do not despair, there is so much help out there to find. Once you love yourself wholly, fully, and completely, you will be able to recognize unacceptable behaviour and put a stop to it.

    I know what it is like to be in such a difficult emotional dark state that it seems like there is no real answer. I know how difficult it is to get out of bed, and live when your heart is broken. I know sometimes things feel hopeless, and you may want to quit, and I am here to tell you are not alone. You matter and you are meant to impact this world. You need to rise like a phoenix from the ashes and keep going. Ask for help? Call someone. There are so many people who are willing to be there for you and love you. You have to know that you have a purpose, and someone needs your hugs and your love. Someone needs your compassion, kindness, and beauty. Please do not give up. There is always someone who needs you because you matter. I know the pain of loneliness and carrying trauma, so I understand how it feels, but I am here to tell you, you can, and you will overcome it if you just believe. I have spent time learning to love the little girl in myself. I journal, listen to her, love her, and give her a voice. I have given back to myself the love that I lost early on. Today, I am the most important person in my life. I do self-care, and I love myself enough to recognize unacceptable behaviour, and now I am able to advocate for myself in my relationships. I always ask myself what the most important thing is for me and based on that I make my decisions. If I hurt someone's feelings because I cannot help them, I apologize but I always have to do what is right for me first. I set boundaries, and say this behaviour is unacceptable to me or it is not okay for you to say that to me. You teach people how to treat you, and you have to stand up for yourself and tell people no, you cannot cross this boundary. Today,

I focus on being the mother that my children need me to be by being present, correcting them, and loving them unconditionally. The Dalai Lama says, *"Our deepest fear is not that we are inadequate. Our deepest fear is that we are powerful beyond measure. It is our light, not our darkness, that most frightens us."* So, take a leap of faith, you are amazing and know you have beautiful bright shining light inside you.

REFLECTIONS

REFLECTIONS

… OVERCOMING THE LOWEST MOMENT IN MY LIFE

REFLECTIONS

Tamar Medford

Tamar Medford is a Neuro Change Method Master Practitioner, Founder of The Road Forward, best-selling Author, and Host of The Road Beyond Recovery Podcast. Since overcoming a 20-year battle with drugs and alcohol, she has dedicated her life to empowering those in recovery to change their beliefs systems and develop growth mindsets. Her mission is to help people master their minds, overcome their limiting beliefs, and create a life so good for themselves they never want to go back to their old way of living.

For more information visit her website:
https://theroadforward.ca/

Pain to Purpose

BY TAMAR MEDFORD
CANADA

LIQUID GOLD

As I sat on the floor looking down at the bottle of pills in my hand, tears streamed down my face, and all I could think was, "How did things get this bad?" According to society, I had everything I needed to live a happy and fulfilled life, or so I thought. I was married, had a home, a nice car, a sweet dog, and people who loved me, but despite all that, I felt as though there was no place for me in this world…I felt alone. I had completely lost my identity, and I felt as though there was no way out. All I saw was darkness. This was the moment that brought me to my knees. I have never been a religious person, but out of complete desperation, I uttered the words, "God, I need your help." It was at that moment that the universe answered my prayers.

Life wasn't always filled with darkness for me; in fact, I had a fantastic childhood. I grew up in a loving family environment and had all the opportunities in the world to create the life I wanted for myself. I watched my dad chase his dream as he worked hard to support our family, and my mum stayed home and cared for my brother and me. One would assume that our lives were perfect, and from the outside, it certainly looked that way. However, the reality was that our family had problems just like everyone else's did, and these problems would eventually begin to shape my limiting beliefs and fears.

In my teens, you could feel the tension developing between my parents. My dad spent a lot of time at work because he loved what he did. He was chasing his dream, a trait that I would eventually pick up as well. During that time, I didn't realise that my dad also suffered from depression, something he hid very well. Oh, and yes, this was something else that I would inherit. My dad and I were very close when I was young, and the harder he worked, the less time we spent together. I was always looking for his approval. I knew he was always proud of me, but part of me wanted to hear him say it, and when that didn't happen, I felt rejected. With any accomplishment I achieved, he would tell me that I could always do better. This was when my perfectionism started to creep in.

When I couldn't get the attention, I was seeking from my dad, I started to look for it through all my other relationships, especially with boys. I remember feeling so out of place in high school. I was terribly shy and felt as though I didn't fit in. Then, one afternoon while I was walking home, I remember getting teased by a couple of older boys. They laughed at me and said I had a big butt and looked like a boy with my short hair. I was utterly devastated and ran home crying. I looked at myself in the mirror and wondered what was wrong with me. I needed a way to gain more confidence, and I would find that missing puzzle piece shortly after.

At the age of fourteen, I found the solution to all my problems: alcohol. It was the one thing that gave me ease and comfort. It transformed me into the confident, outgoing and charismatic person I had always thought others wanted me to be. That desperate desire for approval started to slip away, and it became my perfect escape. My inability to handle my emotions led me to discover a solution that would numb my feelings. When I drank, my world changed from black and white to colour. I felt alive and in control for the first time in my life.

The confidence that alcohol gave me transformed my world. It provided the courage I needed to seek comfort in relationships where I had been too shy before. Being in a relationship meant that I was worthy and loved. My perception of love was that it came from an external source, and I never realised that I had to develop love from within myself.

My desire for approval caused me to bounce from one relationship to another, often not ending one before jumping into the next. Alcohol made this incredibly easy.

My early drinking days were a lot of fun, but I quickly learned that I could become addicted to anything that gave me pleasure or allowed me to avoid my feelings and emotions. I wasn't afraid to put any sort of mind-altering substance into my body, no matter how harmful it was. I started using lighter drugs like marijuana, acid and speed in my teenage years, but this would only progress into hard drugs as I got older.

In my mid-twenties, my addiction escalated. I was partying with a friend one night when I was presented with the opportunity to try crack cocaine for the first time. I had always been curious about it but never knew anyone who sold it. As I inhaled this new substance into my lungs, I suddenly felt invincible. My senses were heightened, and the buzz I felt from the booze I had just consumed vanished. I felt in total control, and it was a wonderful feeling. I had just found a solution that would allow me to drink more alcohol and not suffer the consequences of a blackout. Unfortunately, I had never been very good at knowing when it was time to stop. The reality was that once I started, I couldn't stop. I would often wake up, not knowing how I even got home.

My addiction only got worse. After a week-long bender that left me incredibly sleep-deprived and weak, I slipped a disk in my back at work, which landed me on disability for three months. The combination of the government paying me to stay home and prescribing me painkillers did not result in a positive income. Not only did I get addicted to painkillers, but now I would have the time and financial freedom to get high as often as I wanted.

This was a very dark period in my life. I wound up in places where someone like me, with a good upbringing, should never end up. I woke up in strange homes, used with people I didn't know, and pulled scams to get the money required to feed my habit. Remaining employed became a challenge, and I felt as though my life was starting to fall apart. I felt depressed and emotionally unstable. Everything that I was consuming to try and fill the void inside myself had stopped working. Although I was never really by myself during this time, I felt empty, alone and unloved. I didn't know if I even wanted to exist anymore.

HOPELESS & EMPTY

Being a young adult, naturally, I felt as though the solution to my loneliness was to throw myself into a relationship. Up until this point, I had used men to have fun and get what I needed. As an active alcoholic and drug addict, the morals and values I had been raised with didn't exist. Although it makes me feel sick to say this today, I even got into a relationship with a married man who used to pay me money for small sexual acts to feed my habits. This only made me feel worse inside. You know those people you read about and think to yourself, "How could someone even do that?" Well, I can now share from experience that when you are not in your right mind and suffer from the disease of addiction, you will do anything to escape your reality.

Thinking that love would make things all better, I decided to give this long-term relationship concept a try. Of course, it wasn't a surprise that I would end up attracting someone just like me. I spent the next four years in a relationship that tore me apart mentally, physically and emotionally. I spent weekend after weekend wondering if my partner would come home. Typically, after his payday, he would disappear and get high all weekend until he was out of money and had to stop. He would always come crawling home begging for forgiveness.

Being with an addict can be incredibly difficult because the reality is that we aren't actually bad people; we just do bad things. We have good intentions, and when we say we're sorry most of the time, we genuinely mean it. The tricky part is that when we can get high once again, all those promises we made are forgotten. Up until this point, I had been the one breaking those promises, and it wasn't until I was on the receiving end that I realised how destructive this behaviour was to the loved one of an addict. My heart was being ripped out repeatedly every time he broke his promise to get better. I so desperately wanted to believe that he would change.

I often sat at home alone crying, wondering how someone could confess their love for me yet leave me alone, financially broke and feeling completely abandoned. I started to wonder what I had done to deserve this kind of treatment. Was there something wrong with me? Being with an addict was an emotional rollercoaster that was hard to get off. The bad times were always followed by a short period of bliss and happiness. These happy times would always minimise the pain periodically. It was easy to fall back into the thinking that maybe this time it would be different. Perhaps this time, he meant what he said, and he would change. But, unfortunately, these moments of peace were very short-lived, and the chaos and hurt would inevitably return and continue to get worse.

Although I was no stranger to addiction myself, I sat on my high horse during this time, thinking I was better than him. My co-dependency even led me to believe that I would be the one to save him. For four years, I watched my partner destroy his life, and in the process, I also tore apart my own. The debt we accumulated as a result of our addictions made things unmanageable. I felt myself slipping into the darkness because I just couldn't see the light anymore. When my depression set in, the solution came in a bottle, yet this only made things worse. Each morning when I opened my eyes, all I could think of was the desire to end my suffering for good.

Looking back, I now realise that my inability to handle the sight of blood was probably a good thing because it stopped me from being able to use a razor blade to harm myself. I figured that the consumption of drugs and alcohol might do the trick, or maybe some pills. I now believe that although a massive part of me wanted to die, the universe had alternate plans, and so I was never successful in my attempts. I knew that to change, I had to escape this relationship I found myself clinging so desperately to.

Four years after it all started, I finally gained enough courage to leave. I packed up some of my partner's stuff and made the call for him to come to pick it up. That night when he came home, I was met with a physical beating that left me bruised and battered. After it was all over, I called 911 and spent the rest of the evening giving my statement to the police. Having someone I loved assault me left me feeling alone, scared and very unloved. I started to entertain the idea that maybe I was a waste of space, and that this world would be a better place without me.

I spent the next two months drinking and using cocaine in isolation. Other than going to work to pay my bills, I had no desire to live. I felt numb and emotionless. I had hoped that I would just overdose and die, but unfortunately, that never happened. Instead, every morning I would wake up only to endure the pain once again. My life felt meaningless, and I hated who I had become.

After locking myself away for nearly two months, I decided to climb out of my large pot of pity and explore the outside world. For the past two months, my life had consisted of waking up hungover, going to work, coming home to eat, drink and do lines of cocaine as I sat behind my desk and played solitaire on my computer. This cycle was on rinse and repeat. I was exhausted, and I knew that I was in big trouble if something didn't change soon. Obviously, I had developed a high tolerance over the years because I often wondered why I couldn't just die already.

As I started to present myself to the land of the living again, I began to make small steps in the right direction. I reconnected with my high school best friend and started dating a guy I worked with. Things were looking up, and the darkness I had been so consumed by slowly began to lift. In my experience, people enter our lives for a reason. The combination of these relationships developing right when I needed them the most was not a coincidence. I knew deep down inside that there would be no way out for me if I didn't change. I would either die of some horrible accident, overdose or commit suicide.

I decided that if I was going to turn my life around, I should probably start by doing what others before me had done, and so I got married. You see, I still had this idea that love came from an external source, and if this was the norm in society, so be it. Gary and I worked together, and so our relationship developed quickly. I'm pretty sure he was also an alcoholic, and to be honest, that worked out nicely for me because we never went anywhere without a drink in our hand. Although he was a heavy drinker, just like myself, he had made it clear in the early stages of our relationship that he wouldn't tolerate drug use which probably helped more than I realised back then.

Early married life was great, but my husband and I slowly started to grow apart as the years went on. The only times we ever had an engaging conversation was when he was drinking. Another area that affected me deeply was that he had also struggled with a porn addiction. The combination of the two left me feeling unloved and depressed. I would often wonder if I wasn't attractive enough, or maybe I had just gained too much weight for him to want me. I didn't understand how things had gotten this bad so quickly! Not only that, but our debt had gotten to an unmanageable point. The hole we had dug for ourselves seemed almost impossible to escape from.

I started having dark thoughts again, and at one point, I went to visit my husband at work to tell him I was going to end my life so that he could receive our life insurance benefits and move on. I meant every word because the anxiety I faced due to our financial troubles affected my work performance. He was in total shock and couldn't believe what I had just told him. Thankfully, he took my plea seriously because he began putting in some extra hours to help lessen the financial burden. Unfortunately, this only aided our situation temporarily because our drinking was a bigger priority, so our condition worsened, and so did our relationship.

Being married and feeling so alone felt terrible for me. I had no idea how to handle my emotions because I had spent most of my adult life drinking to numb them out. As a result, I had no idea how to express myself without bursts of anger, and the thoughts of suicide only got worse. Through the advice of a friend of mine, I finally went to see a doctor and asked for help. I was diagnosed with depression and quickly medicated. This was a step in the right direction, but there was still a significant problem I had never thought about addressing alcohol. I was an alcoholic, and yet it's something I never wanted to look at because of the stigma associated with it. From the outside, it looked as though we had it all together, but the reality was totally different and one that reflected the life of an alcoholic closely.

Alcohol was my solution for everything, and so to no big surprise, when I was taken off my medication a year later, the alcohol took hold again and off I went. My weight escalated to just over 215 lbs, my marriage was worse than ever, and we were on the brink of bankruptcy. Alcohol was always my go-to because it always worked. That was until it didn't any longer. I saw no way out, and I no longer had the desire to live. I was tired of hurting the people I loved, so I decided I would end this madness.

When I first started this story, I mentioned that moment in time that changed everything. This was that moment. As I sat there on the floor with my bottle of pills, I knew it was now or never. I was desperate to end the suffering I not only caused myself but also caused others. Good thing the universe had different plans. I stared at the bottle of pills but somehow couldn't bring myself to take them. Something came over me at that moment, and I made a choice to stop living the way I had for so long. Call it divine intervention or what you will, but I realised that it was time to take responsibility for the life I had created and get out of my pity pot. At that moment, as I prayed for help, the universe listened.

NEW LIFE

In January 2012, at the age of thirty-six years old, I made a choice to change my life. I still didn't realise that alcohol was a problem, but the decision I made then would set the ball in motion and what followed was a truly incredible experience. My rock bottom was the moment I decided to stop digging. I was severely depressed, weighed 215 lbs / 97.5kg, was unhappily married, financially bankrupt and had absolutely no desire to live. The crazy part is that it could have been much worse.

I assumed that my depression and anxiety came about because I was overweight and unhappily married, so I decided to do what most people do in the New Year and get myself a gym membership. I also decided that I couldn't do this alone, so I hired a personal trainer. Unknown at the time, the personal trainer I hired was someone in recovery. This relationship would ultimately lead me towards making the best decision of my life; I just wasn't aware of it yet.

When I sat down with my trainer for the first time, we realised we knew each other from high school, so a friendship had developed quickly. I was a model student with my usual all-in mentality, so as you can imagine, I jumped in with both feet, well, my whole body, actually! I worked out six to seven days a week and ate chicken, broccoli and rice daily. I had one cheat meal per week and kept to the plan. Now I realise how much this all or nothing mentality mirrored my drug and alcohol addiction very closely. Many people who give up one addiction often replace it with another. I'm just grateful this was a much healthier one.

I still had one obstacle, however, and that was alcohol. I created a plan to have only nine beers per week, consuming those from Friday to Sunday. It was brilliant as far as I was concerned! Once I finished my daily beverages, I would ask my husband to take me home, where I then drank half a bottle of cold medicine to pass out and fall asleep. When Monday rolled around, and I had to report my weekly food journal, I remember wanting to shout from the rooftops that I had only had nine beers all weekend. I would eventually learn that this could be a sign you have a problem. Apparently, most people do not feel the need to brag about how much they did or did not drink. This seems to only be a trait of those who have a problem and feel the need to convince others that they don't.

As good as my plan was, this would only last for so long. I had filled my time up with gym visits, training sessions and boot camps so that I didn't have time to revisit my old life. This also gave me the false perception that I had kicked my drinking problem and was in total control. I swapped one addiction for another, until I was presented with the opportunity of a weekend holiday with my husband. My intention was to have one bottle of wine throughout the entire weekend, but that was short-lived in the first hour after finishing that first bottle. I don't remember much of the rest of the weekend, but it was then that I knew I needed help when it came to my drinking.

Shortly before my weekend away, my personal trainer had planted the bug in my ear that she was in recovery and that if I ever needed help, she would be there. At the time, I laughed off the suggestion because I didn't think I was an alcoholic, to begin with. I mean, I was only drinking nine beers per weekend, and no alcoholic could pull that off, right?

On the16th June 2012, was the last time I had a drink. I was terrified of the idea of never having another drink because, since the age of fourteen, it was all I knew. But as I laid in bed wholly hungover and coming out of another blackout, I sucked up my pride and texted the words, "I need help."

As I embarked on this new chapter in my life, I started to put one foot in front of the other. I discovered that nothing went according to my plan when I attempted to control outcomes and the people around me. So, the first thing I had to do was surrender to the idea that I had a problem and that I didn't have to discover the solution alone. This is one of the most challenging parts of getting sober or making life-changing decisions, for that matter. When we struggle to see our own reality, it's hard to know what to change. There is no shame in asking for help and guidance.

The first step I had to take was writing out my life story. This is an exercise that I recommend to all my clients needing to make significant life changes. I started to write out my story from the time I took that first drink and wrote until I had hit my rock bottom. The next step was to read it out loud to someone I trusted. Here is where the surrendering part comes in. As I read each word out loud, it quickly became apparent how incredibly unmanageable my life had become. It was shocking to be honest how I made it out of those twenty plus years alive. Now that I saw my actual reality and the life I had created, I could start to make the past right.

The second step was to realise that I didn't have to walk this path alone. Here is where faith came into play. I had been trying to run the show called my life for so long, and it wasn't working out too well. I was told that it was ok to "Let go and let god." In the world of recovery, the saying "let go and let god" means that you can let God, or any other higher power of your choosing worry about the stuff you can't control. In other words, letting go and letting God do the work instead. The word God didn't sit well with me at first because I wasn't religious, and I had always been under the assumption that if there was a God, I wouldn't be where I was in the first place. The reality was that I made it out of a life of addiction alive, so there had to be something watching over me. It was up to me to come up with what that higher power or spirit was called. I wrote out what I wanted my higher power to look like, which was a great exercise.

The tricky part came after I took the first couple of steps, which was also very humbling to be honest. I had to write out a list of everyone I had any resentment towards and had ever harmed in any way. As you can imagine, the list was long to start off with. This is now an exercise I do once a year because it allows me to always see my part in every situation. It also allows you to see patterns in your behaviours. More often than not, I realised it's my expectations of others that got me in trouble. After I had created this long list of who I resented or harmed, what the resentment was and what insecurity it affected within myself, I had to identify the role I played. Again, I read this inventory to someone I trusted, and the whole process took about four hours. I felt absolutely drained afterwards, but it was as though a massive weight had been lifted off my shoulders. I gained a new sense of freedom.

Once I had completed this inventory, I knew what I had to start working on to better myself and my relationships. I also recognised where my fear of being alone and being abandoned played a massive part in my actions and behaviours. Again, it came down to my inability to handle my emotions. I cried more in that first year of sobriety than I had my entire life, but I had the tools to work through those emotions for the first time. There was a sense of empowerment experienced when I learned to recognise that in all our experiences, we can't control the behaviours of others, but we can choose how we respond. We can also set boundaries in relationships where maybe enabling was part of the dynamic previously.

Now it was time to clean up 'my side of the street.' It was apparent to me the damage I had done. I had long conversations with friends and family and owned up to what I had done. This also allowed them to say their part, and it wasn't always easy to hear, but I listened. This was the start of mending these relationships and moving forward. I knew the words sorry wouldn't cut it; I had to show people I was serious about changing. The point was to do my part and own my mistakes; how people responded to that was none of my business.

My first year of sobriety wasn't easy, and I lost everything but gained so much more. My marriage ended, and I went financially bankrupt. The only material possessions I had was a dresser, bookshelf, and a bed. I was grateful to still be employed at the job I had held down for the past five years so at least I had an income have a good job, and a friend of mine allowed me to rent a room in her home. I felt like the luckiest person alive at that moment.

This is where the last steps to building my foundation in early recovery came in. I learned what humility was and how to live a more honest life. I had to create a mindfulness routine and develop a spiritual practice. I also knew that I needed to help others. This was the perfect opportunity to slowly let go of my self-centredness and pass on what was so freely given to me. Believe it or not, when we help others, it can end up helping us more. Anytime I worked with another alcoholic, I forgot my problems and only focussed on the person I was helping, therefore allowing me to stay out of my own head. Being stuck in your own head is a dangerous place to be for someone in recovery.

The definition of recovery is gaining control over something that was lost, and anytime I drank or got high I lost control and made bad decisions that impacted my life in a negative way. I lost a lot over my twenty years of addiction. By getting sober, I gained the opportunity to do a lot of self-analyses in the process and learned how I could help others through my experience. I discovered how to live a healthier lifestyle and even lost seventy-five pounds in that first year. For the first time in my life, I didn't feel like I was sucking the life out of those around me. My parents didn't have to worry anymore, and I started making better choices. I was becoming a productive member of society, and I was also beginning to drop the shame around being in recovery.

Here are the steps I took to build a foundation in my life.

1. **Write out your story. (Surrender)**
   - ✓ You can start from the moment you first remember experiencing the struggle or behaviours you want to change, or you can go even further back if you'd like to dig into the reasons why you may have started to begin with. The point is to recognise patterns or unmanageability.

2. **Develop a form of faith.**
   - ✓ If you struggle with this concept, write out what you'd like a higher power to look like. Does this look like love, light, energy or maybe even a support group? Just know you don't have to walk this journey alone.

3. **Inventory (Resentments and Recognising your part)**
   - ✓ Create a list of who you're resentful at.
   - ✓ List all the reasons why you have this resentment.
   - ✓ Think of the insecurities it triggers within you.
   - ✓ Identify the part you played in the resentment. Was it your expectations? Have you been enabling other people's behaviour? Reading this to someone else can often help you identify your part more clearly.

4. **Create a routine including mindfulness practices.**
   - ✓ Add a form of meditation to your daily routine.
   - ✓ In the areas you have limiting beliefs create affirmations that are the opposite.

- ✓ In times of turbulence, take three deep breaths and think before responding.
5. **Become other people centred.**
    - ✓ This is nothing better than helping others to get out of your own head. Say or do something kind for someone when you can!

MY NEW REALITY

The sad reality for those who have overcome addiction is that many do not make it. I consider myself to be one of the lucky few who embrace a new life of recovery and gain the desire to learn and become better through my mistakes. After about five years of being sober and not having the desire to end my life, I still felt as though something was missing. I felt as though I was on this planet to fulfil a greater purpose.

I was full of gratitude, but each morning I would wake up and not feel satisfied with my career or that I still didn't really have an idea of what I wanted to be when I grew up. I was just living and not actually thriving. I always had the feeling as though I was meant for more, but I had absolutely no idea what that more was or how to find it. I had been taught that I should always be grateful for what I had, and I certainly was, but there was a piece missing, and I knew I had to find it.

In early 2019 I started to do some self-analysis. Other than my recovery, I hadn't done much in terms of personal development. I had always been too afraid to invest in myself because my history dictated that I never finished what I started. Here is the reality and what I see now, through being more personally aware. I already had the skills I needed to create the life of my dreams. All throughout my addiction and suicidal times, I was persistent, resilient, and incredibly resourceful. Now, if I could put those skills towards something I was passionate about, just imagine the change I could create.

I love helping people get sober because when you see the light go on in someone's eyes, it is a fantastic feeling when they realise, they can change. I knew that those skills came from surrounding myself with people who were sober and had what I wanted, so I figured that if I did the same in terms of learning to become an entrepreneur, I would achieve similar results.

The next step was that I had to educate myself and invest in some personal development, so I decided to take a Life Coaching Course and become a Performance Consultant. I had no college education, but I knew that with my life experience, I would do great at being able to relate to the adversity people faced, especially at the hands of addiction. I've realised that when I invest in my personal development, my rate of return is usually tripled! Not only that, but I get the opportunity to be a student of the work myself.

Now that I had the support I needed, I decided it was time to discover my purpose. I have read many self-help and inspirational books over the past few years, and the common theme in those who have found success was that they found a purpose greater than themselves. Everything they did aligned with their purpose, and they had the grit to move through any roadblocks. Discovering this made me realise that I possessed the skills required to create a more purpose-driven life because of what I had been through and the fact that I made it out alive.

I found my purpose through a Japanese concept called Ikigai. In English, it translates roughly to "a reason for being" or "the reason we wake up in the morning." To discover your Ikigai, you need to answer four questions.

1. What do you love?
2. What are you good at?
3. What could you get paid for? Or What is your calling?
4. What does the world need more of?

I wrote down everything I could think of under each heading and, when I was finished, highlighted the things that aligned with one another or resonated with me. I also did a little extra exercise, and that was texting three friends and asking them the question, "If you came to me for advice on anything, what would that advice be? What do you see are my strengths." I added this extra exercise because we often do not see our own strengths like others do. I added the responses to my list and used these as a pick me up if I was having a bad day. This exercise benefited me in more than one way because it served as positive affirmations written by others.

Discovering my purpose also made decision making a whole lot easier! If I had to decide between option A & option B, I would ask myself which one aligned with the life I wanted to create for myself. It also helped in setting boundaries. I had always been a people pleaser, and so often, I would commit to things out of feeling obligated to do it. Living that way only led to more resentments in my life. 'No' can be a powerful word when we learn to use it properly, and I haven't lost a friendship yet due to saying 'no' to something that does not align with what I'm genuinely passionate about.

Successful people also possessed resilience and a strong belief in their ability to achieve their goals. So, to do this, I knew I had to get rid of the limiting beliefs that held me back. In my early sobriety, I assumed that my past would always follow me around in a negative way. Never did I imagine that my past would become the key to my success. All this time, life had been training me for this very moment. Once I realised this, I learned to start letting go of the limiting beliefs that no longer served me.

I did this through a process of challenging your beliefs, followed by belief revision. First, I wrote down all the limiting beliefs and negative self-talk that had held me back in life. Next, I started to look for evidence that contradicted these beliefs. Oftentimes it was just a matter of asking myself the simple question of, "Do I know this belief to be 100% true and factual?" Most of the time, the answer was no. These were just stories I told myself after feeling an emotion. Following this, I then wrote down the opposite of my limiting belief. In other words, I wrote down the belief I would like to possess. I created a list of habits that those with that particular belief would practice, and one by one, I started to implement those new habits into my daily routine.

Here are some of the new habits I started to incorporate into my daily routine.

1. **Visualisation**
   - ✓ I wrote out where I'd like to be in five years from now as though it already happened. I would reach this each morning or spend ten minutes in silence imagining it as though it was true. When you visualise, it's essential to dig up feelings and truly experience everything as though you are living through it.

2. **Daily Affirmations**
   - ✓ Write out a list of positive affirmations or positive statements as though they are already true and read these daily. This is great to shift your negative self-talk as well.

3. **Well-Being Journaling (Write this out daily!)**
   - ✓ Three positive characteristics
   - ✓ Three things I'm grateful for
   - ✓ Three things I'm excited about
   - ✓ Wins for the day
   - ✓ (Create your intention for the following day) When I wake up in the morning, I will…

4. **Meditation**
   - ✓ Guided meditation has always worked best for me. Use an app like Calm or Insight Timer, or choose your own kind of meditation

5. **Organisational Skills**
   - ✓ I plan everything important to me during the first part of the day! That way, if life gets in the way, I know I've done what I wanted to do.
   - ✓ I create a list of daily tasks, weekly tasks and later tasks.
   - ✓ I schedule everything in my Google calendar and colour code it. This makes it easy to see how my week is scheduled out.

- ✓ For any task I need to complete, I allot a specific amount of time to it. When you give 30-minute job 3 hours, it will take you 3 hours, so schedule the 30-minutes and stay focused until you are done.

6. **Read for 10 minutes a day**
   - ✓ I make sure I read for at least 10 minutes per day, if not longer. During the day, I read self-help or educational reading, and at night before bed, I switch to a romance or memoir. I keep it light in the evening to slow my thinking down and get a good night's sleep!

7. **Learn something new daily**
   - ✓ Each day I make a point of learning something new. I am always taking a course, watching a video or webinar and feeding my brain. Perhaps you might like to start listening to a podcast. Choose your own preferred learning style.

8. **Appreciation Calls**
   - ✓ This was taught to me, and I've done it daily for over a year now! Pick a friend that has trouble staying positive or wants some additional accountability. Leave each other a three-minute voice memo or voicemail (I highly recommend the memo, so you don't get cut off). Share what you appreciate and what you're grateful for that day.
   - ✓ Then listen to your friend's message and get some added inspiration as well!

9. **Get a good night's sleep!**
   - ✓ I used to take sleep for granted. Now, I get at least seven to eight hours of sleep per night. In fact, I go to bed and wake up at the same time daily, no matter what day of the week it is.
   - ✓ When we get enough rest, we make better decisions, period. I can't tell you how many times I've reached for food that made me feel like crap because I was exhausted and needed energy.

- ✓ Being rested also allows you to handle your emotions more effectively.
- ✓ My standard routine to ensure I get a good night's sleep is to turn off all electronics at least an hour before bed. I then read for about thirty to sixty minutes to wind down and follow that up with a meditation or recorded hypnotherapy session to which I fall asleep too. The key for me has been to wind down at least an hour or two before I want to fall asleep.

People often ask me how I manage to get so much done in a day, and to that, I reply with the answers I've shared above. There is no secret, just the desire to take care of myself whenever possible because my purpose is so strong, I will do what it takes to continue to follow that mission. Having a good mindfulness routine and being consistent with that routine has made all the difference in my day-to-day life. Developing this routine while still working a full-time job also helped me transition into the entrepreneur part of my journey.

When Covid hit, my days travelling for my corporate job ended. I now worked from home, so I decided it was time to officially start my coaching business because I was no longer commuting or spending a lot of time at the airport. I knew that if I grew my business to a point where I could follow my passion full time, I had to be very intentional with my time.

I started by writing out how I spent my day. This included tracking how much time I wasted on tasks that weren't aligned with my goals or purpose. I even used the app on my phone to tell me how much time I spent on social media. This data resulted in my putting a limit on my phone, and if I went over that allotted time, the app would turn off. As I started to eliminate anything that didn't align with the future I wanted to create, I began to replace those things with stuff I enjoyed.

Doing what I loved first thing in the morning got me excited to start my day. In fact, during the period I was still working my corporate job, I would often rise at 3:30am just so I had enough time to work on my side projects. I even wrote two best-selling books in less than a year using this structure. My first book was called "Hope Elevated", where I shared my journey in overcoming addiction. Being vulnerable about my journey in such an open way fuelled my desire to help others even more. So much so that it inspired me to write my second book called "Beyond Recovery." Self-publishing my first two books gave me the confidence I needed to believe in my abilities to accomplish things I always thought to be impossible.

Through all that I have accomplished since overcoming my demons, I have created a life so good for myself that I never want to go back to my old way of living. I never think about drinking, nor do I want to end my life. That isn't to say I don't have my dark days anymore because they do creep up from time to time. I still struggle with depression occasionally, but the difference between my past and now is that today I can always see the light in the distance no matter how dark things get. I have learned to handle my emotions and embrace them.

It all started with building a foundation and recognising the areas in my life I had to improve. Then I had to have the willingness to change because change without action is only a dream. I was tired of settling for a life lacking true joy and fulfilment, so I decided to never settle for anything less. I had to learn how to get out of my comfort zone and appreciate that the discomfort of trying something new meant growth. I discovered my purpose, and as a result of that discovery, I get to live a purpose-driven life where I do what I love. And finally, I had to believe that my past and the experiences that I had been through was a means to creating the life I was truly meant to live.

Action steps to accomplishing your dreams.

1. Develop a support network
2. Discover your purpose
3. Invest in yourself!
4. Eliminate limiting beliefs
5. Know that you can thrive!

And if you wish to speak with me regarding any element of what I have written and feel that I can help you, then please reach out to me at **tamar@theroadforward.ca** or visit **www.theroadforward.ca**. I look forward to connecting with you.

REFLECTIONS

REFLECTIONS

Sandra Chaney

Sandra Chaney is a 7x best-selling author, certified empowerment coach, certified Les Brown Motivational Speaker, non-profit consultant, wife, and mother.

Sandra received Brave, Bold and Beautiful award for women leaders who are not built to break; the Humanitarian Award from Trinity International University of Ambassadors for being an Extraordinary Leader; and the Fruit of Her Hand award from The Black Church and Domestic Violence Institute for women who have risen above their circumstances to make a difference in their community.

Sandra lives her life by this motto: "Everything I do, say and offer the world will come from a deep place of love!"

Visit **https://sandrachaney.com** to learn more.

When I wake up, I choose ME

BY SANDRA CHANEY
USA

"Ms. Mizell, do you know where you are? Do you know why you are here?" These are the questions which greeted me as I woke up in the hospital. 'Why am I still here, I wondered? I can't even do that right' I thought. Then I heard what I heard as a child: "You will never amount to anything. You will be no better than the bums in the street." I remember crying and feeling like such a failure. WHEW! How did I get here? Well, come along with me as I travel back down memory lane and I will tell you.

I am a native New Yorker and a sixties baby. My earliest remembrance of chaos in my life begins around age six. I grew up in a household where I experienced emotional and some physical abuse. I did not have a great relationship with my parents. As a child, I often felt unloved and unwanted. My mother never said the words "I love you." I would dream about what it would be like to hear her say those words.

Getting yelled at or receiving beatings were the norm for me. Seeing my parents fighting was the norm for me. Seeing my parents drinking was the norm for me. I never had true friends because they could never come over. Our house was a house of secrets. I truly felt like Cinderella. Do you know that story? She lived with her step-mum and sisters. They were mean to her, and she did everything, the cooking, cleaning, etc. While I did not have to cook and my sisters were NOT mean to me, I was responsible for all the cleaning, laundry, and ironing and whatever else my parents thought I should do. My childhood was not fun. I always felt like I had to figure out how to be a peacemaker or at least find peace amidst the chaos. To find that peace, I started smoking and drinking around the age of thirteen. So much was going on, I just did not know how to cope.

We travelled every summer, when school was out, to visit family. I was always excited because I could not wait to visit my cousins and grandparents, most of all I could not wait to see my favourite cousin. This particular summer would change that feeling. I was nine years old; he was eighteen. He did not mind me tagging along behind him. I followed him everywhere he went. I even hung out with him in his room. As a young girl who trusted him so much that I never gave it much thought when he started to touch me in strange places on my body. The adults and caretakers in my life did not warn me about appropriate and inappropriate touching. He told me it was OK, because "We are family." "After all," he said, "family can do anything they want." I loved him like a brother and believed everything he said. Eventually the touching turned into sexual intercourse, and it did not feel good. I remember complaining of the pain and he told me that it would go away. "Remember, we are family, and we love each other." He made me promise not to tell anyone. This was our secret. I was a kid, so I was excited about having a secret. This went on for several years.

After a while, the family trips stopped. I would never see him again and I never told anyone about our secret. Besides, I didn't think anyone would believe me because we were family after all, right? When I started hitting my teen years, I started to think family protects each other at all costs. Whatever happened behind closed doors, stayed behind closed doors. At the time, I accepted what was said to me as family protecting each other, so I just went on with my life. In the back of my mind, however, I always thought something was not quite right, and as my life went on, I often became agitated and anxious without understanding why. I often had trouble sleeping. I also began engaging in high-risk behaviours such as drinking, smoking and hanging around with dysfunctional people, basically anyone that would allow me to be in their space.

Trying to have some normality in my life during my teen years was hard. I tried to make friends and would accept anyone who wanted me in their space. I never felt like I fitted in anywhere. I always thought I was weird. I did not like how I looked, I felt my hair was too coarse (meaning not straight, fine and shining), thick and dirty, lips and eyes too big. I really struggled with being me. In the midst of abuse and alcoholism in my home, I'm now struggling with how I look. I was very insecure and lacked confidence. I was never affirmed growing up, so I accepted anything and anyone. When I was sixteen, I was sexually assaulted whilst running an errand for my parents.

In New York, you can walk or ride the subway everywhere. I was walking and returning home when I was stopped by these young men. They were hurling sexual innuendos at me at the same time telling me how pretty I was. Next thing I remember was waking up in the back alley of a building with no clothes. I cannot tell you what happened in between because I blacked out. Someone heard me screaming and invited me into their home. I really retreated within myself after that. I blocked out what I did not want to remember. I did the whole reporting, they got arrested, I went to court, and they got time, and guess what? Throughout all of this, I didn't have support from the parents. I was on this journey by myself. Nothing new. This was my life, no emotional support.

I decided at the age of seventeen to leave home. I promised myself I would finish high school and I did. I was seeking peace and I just wanted to feel good about myself. My parents told me basically they were not wasting their money to pay for college and the service won't take me either so, I left home. I found myself in the arms of a pimp. Of course, I did not know that was his profession. All I knew was, he smelled good, looked good and thought I was pretty. Soon enough, I found out it was all a lie. I was being sex trafficked, like the rest of the girls I met, who I thought were his family. It wasn't long before I was arrested. That really was a blessing in disguise. Had I not been arrested I really don't know where I would have ended up or if I would have lived at that time. I saw girls being beaten up and threatened. I was made to watch the abuse being inflicted upon them. I believe it was a way to put fear in me to keep me from running; it worked. Yup, being arrested got me away from that. I never told my parents, because I was so embarrassed and secondly, I felt they would have scolded me. Once again, I retreated within and went about life like nothing ever happened.

I moved to a different state after that to start fresh when I was nineteen. About two years later, I am married with a child. Who does that? I was seeking, as the cliché goes, love in all the wrong places. Once again, someone is paying attention to me, and it really did feel good. He was thirteen years older than me. That was the story of my life. The pimp was eight years older than me. My first real boyfriend was nine years older than me, and I convinced myself that I liked older men. Not true. I just wanted to be loved and feel better about myself. Oh, I forgot, at the time he looked good and smelled good. I was starting to realise I had a pattern and type. They reminded me in some way of my dad. I dated my first husband for a year, moved in with him and then we got married. He did not want to. I planned the whole thing and then told him. I pretty much gave him no choice. I am desperately seeking validation and to be free of pain from somewhere. I was looking to truly live the American dream, a house with a white picket fence and a family. Well, the dream was fast becoming a nightmare.

I decided I wanted a child because I'm still looking for an emotional connection and I wanted to feel good, so I got pregnant. At first it was cool. As time went on, I realised this dream of feeling loved and pain free was not becoming a true reality. My home life reflected my childhood, abuse, and alcoholism. We fought all the time, and I realised I was doing to my son what was done to me. It was an all too familiar space, chaotic. I knew I needed to leave; I was afraid. Although the support I was getting from my then husband was not good, to me it was better than nothing. Besides, the thought of being a single parent scared me. Chaotic was better than nothing. One day, it all changed. We get into an argument and next thing I know I have a gun to my head with my then two-year-old son crying. All I could do was pray. Needless to say, he left and so did I. The one thing I did not want to do was be divorced and a single mother. Again, I'm thinking you just can't do anything right. How did I get here?

Here I was in a state where I didn't know anyone other than a few family members, but even that was a little challenging. I now had to figure out how to navigate being a mum and work. I did not know how to be a mum or at least that is what I thought. I have this amazing human depending on me. I remember telling myself, "Don't screw this up." To say I was depressed is an understatement. Depression is very REAL! I did not really realise I was depressed, and I would walk around saying I am sad, tired or mentally drained. I really thought about going back home and decided against it. Going from one chaotic space to another was not good for me or my child. Every day I got up and did what I needed to do. I did not feel, I didn't even cry, I just went through the motions because I felt I had no choice.

Being alone did not feel good to me, so I ended up getting into a long-term relationship. I was trying to rid myself of the pain and looking for love. I really did not know what that felt like to truly be loved unconditionally. How can I give this to my son when I did not feel it for myself? I had so many questions and I felt like getting into another relationship would answer all my problems. It only made it worse, and of course I just pretended that everything was okay. Pretending became easy for me. I probably should have been in the movies. I was really that good at it, at least that is what I believed. I just fell into a routine and thought this was how my life was supposed to be. Interestingly enough, I again found myself in a space that was all too familiar, chaotic. Life was getting very tiring, and this motherhood thing was too much for me to handle. Something had to give.

My depression was deeper than I knew. If the truth be told, everything I survived growing up was coming to a head. I was probably in my late twenties when I started thinking my life is not worth living. Convinced

I was not a good mother, I asked some family members to take care of my child, so I could get myself together. I was attempting to figure out a way to feel better and find that all elusive unconditional love. During that season of my life, I was divorced, a single parent, a survivor of several abusive relationships, in a relationship that was not good for my soul and working in Corporate America. Everyone who knew me during that season, including colleagues, always complimented me on how strong and put together I looked. Yet on the inside I was so sad and crying. I just wanted to feel good. For those of you reading this who have been through something similar, I am sure you can relate to putting yourself together well on the outside just so you feel good on the inside.

Still searching, I remember being at work one day and deciding to cut all my hair off because I am trying to find a way to feel good about myself. It was as if my hair was weighing me down, so during my lunch hour, I found a barbershop and told the barber to cut it all off. It felt so liberating! It was instant gratification, although at the time, I did not realise it. The other patrons in the shop, mainly men, told me how beautiful I was, and it felt so good. However, when I returned to work the reaction was different. I was told I was being militant, a rebel, which I took in a negative way. Then I went home, and it was not any better. The words from my partner at that time were hurtful. I tried to maintain the feeling from the words of others in the barbershop. I was never given words of affirmation growing up. So, I always looked for my happiness and joy outside of me, only to discover it was already within me all along. I just needed to know that. I felt like cutting my hair off gave me this sense of power, but it was false. When my mum saw my short hair, she took it personally and began to make me feel as if I did this to get back at her. I denied it, but then I wondered if she was right. Was I being truthful with myself?

For readers in America, you may remember a show called "To Tell the Truth?" I think this was a sixties show. In this show three people are introduced, all claiming to be the actual person. Each person is asked their name. They all are giving the same name – pretending to be someone else. In this game, a group of panellists are given permission to ask questions of each challenger. The real person has sworn to give truthful answers and the imposters are allowed to lie. They pretend to be the actual character. Well, to tell the truth, I struggled with knowing who I was. I gave myself permission to lie about my past and pretend to be someone I wasn't. When asked to really talk about myself, it was always difficult. This quest to find out who the real me was, all came to a head. I was about to come face to face with myself in the most awful of ways.

Suicide, in my mind, was the only way to get peace. I did not know another way. At the time, it seemed as if everyone, including my son, would be better off without me. By now, I am functioning in my depression, or at least, that's what I thought. No one talks about mental health at least not back then; we barely talk about it now. Anyway, when I woke up in the hospital, I'm like "Damn, you can't even do that right!" I did question why I was still here. Maybe deep down inside, there was some part of me that really wanted to be here, all I knew was I just wanted the pain to go away.

Attempting suicide was my cry for help. I was too ashamed to ask for help. It was easier to pretend. I was now coming face to face with the real Sandra and the pretend life I had been living. The day I decided to attempt suicide, I was home by myself feeling sad and rethinking everything that had happened in my life. I put on some sad soppy music and started drinking. I think this was the first time I also started to feel because tears were flowing. At that moment, I was not thinking of taking my life, yet I felt like I was worthless. I just kept drinking. The more I drank, the more I wanted the pain to stop. I was getting a headache and went looking for some medicine. I came across a bottle of headache medicine. This is when I got the idea to leave this world. I sat back down on the floor and thought about how I brought my child into a chaotic world, how everything I touched seemed to fail and just how worthless I felt. So, I finished off the six pack of beer and took a bottle of pills. I found myself in the hospital and thus began my journey of healing and finding true unconditional love. Waking up in the hospital and realising

I was still here only reinforced to me that I once again failed. What in the world is happening? I just want to be free.

What's interesting about this was everyone in the hospital was very supportive, whilst I was combative. The emotional support and unconditional love I was seeking started in the hospital. How funny is that? My suicide attempt landed me in an inpatient home for thirty days. Of course, I was resistant and insisted I was good. The good doctors and nurses were not hearing me. To make sure I went through with this process they had one of the house counsellors pick me up and take me to my new home for the next thirty days. It was dark when I got there, so I could not really see what the outside looked like. The inside was a house with furniture and people, who I was not interested in meeting at first. I had to share a room. I felt like I was in jail. The next day I got to see the home from the outside. It was surrounded by beautiful trees, flowers, lots of land and deer. It was where I began my love affair with nature. It was also here that I began to face some things.

Getting used to a different routine without chaos at the centre of everything was a little challenging. Sharing my feelings with others who cared was also strange to me, and to get genuine hugs and smiles was definitely foreign. I had to first figure out if these people were being real and not fake. Over time, I found out they were real. I was beginning to sense what peace may feel like. There was no yelling, arguing, fighting, or drunk people in this space. I had to get used to a process and a routine that would allow for some self-care. Every day I was learning things in the group and individually. One of the things I learned was that forgiving me, yes ME, myself, was paramount and part of my healing process. It was easy for me to say the words, however the manifestation of those words took years. What I realised now, is that it is a process. There is no overnight fix. We've got to feel our way through the pain, hurt and acknowledge the shame in order to begin healing.

Being in that space forced me to come face to face with how much "stuff" I had been carrying and what it was doing to me. This is where the rubber meets the road and I had to tell the truth. My life was being turned upside down, from finances to relationships and everything in between. Everything was coming to a head, and I was forced to face the reasons why. I was secretly still carrying the pain and hurt of not feeling loved, the shame of being sexually attacked at nine years old by my cousin and then at sixteen; pretending to still have it all together, when inside I felt so inadequate and very insecure. In the past I kept asking God for a change from the inside out, but discovered I was not as ready as I thought. There is a Sam Cooke song titled "A Change Is Gonna Come". In it he talks about being born in a little tent and always running like a river. I had to face the tents (shame, feeling unloved, not loving self, insecurities) that I was living in and rid myself of them.

Forgiveness for blaming myself for things that happen to me was my first step in beginning my healing journey. By facing myself, I went to my secret place within me. In my secret place, I learned to start where the pain first began. I went to where the pain first began, and I allowed myself to feel. That was so painful, and it hurt. I cried so much, but it was necessary in order to be free. I also forgave the people, including my parents, realizing that I may never hear an apology for them. It was okay, because I was choosing to love myself, love unconditionally and live my best life. Walking in my truth was something else I needed to do.

As a part of my truth, I realised that being a survivor of domestic violence and sexual assault gave me a place to hide from my depression. Of course, I did not see that at the time. I mean who would not be depressed after dealing with that? Besides, I had never heard of anyone saying I am a survivor or conqueror of depression, so I am changing that now "I am a survivor or conqueror of domestic violence". It was easy to wear that as a badge of honour, surviving domestic violence. That too fed my need for validation and it really was easy to hide behind that. Depression never came up in my conversations. I was too embarrassed – besides, how can I be a survivor of domestic violence and be depressed and I wondered why no one ever talked about it? Then, I realised it must start with 'self'. I am very grateful for my counsellor who initiated that conversation. This was my first lesson in breathing. Allowing myself to become vulnerable enough to open my heart and share my pain. It at least starts a conversation and helps me to peel back another layer of my onion., but I had to keep the conversation going as part of my self-care.

Here is how I kept that 'conversation with self' going:

1. I entered therapy. Of course, it was a part of my treatment plan, but I knew this was what I needed. So, I participated fully in the process. Please go to therapy, if necessary. It really is a good thing. I will say this, having the RIGHT therapist is important. Having someone to help you navigate your thoughts and feelings is vital to your mind, body, and spirit.

2. I acknowledged that I really was depressed. That meant I needed to be vulnerable; I needed to open my heart; I needed to be honest with myself; and I needed to put voice to it and not hide from it. You cannot heal what you won't acknowledge. If you are unaware or unsure check in with a professional to see where you are.

3. I get at least seven hours of sleep a night and I take naps when I can. I found when I did not get enough sleep through the week it affected my emotional state and how I handled things. Over time the effects of no sleep become magnified with everything else going on. I am important! You are important. Get some good sleep. It works wonders!

4. I started visiting the beach or just being near water. I can exhale and just be. I can just let go and release.

5. Just getting outside in the sun. The vitamin D rays from the sun feel so good. Get out in the sun. Just get out of the house. Do something for you.

6. I exercise, I do yoga, regularly; I move my body. I love to dance too. I take dance breaks in the middle of the day because I love music. When you move your body, it clears stagnant energy.

7. Remember to BREATHE! Your breath will save you! I make a conscious effort to feel my breath. That means, I must stop what I'm doing to check in with me and my breath helps me with that.

I will never say this journey was easy for me. After attempting suicide and landing myself in an inpatient facility, I decided, there must be a reason why I am still here. It was a very challenging journey. Some days, I wanted to give up, yet I kept going. I had a son that needed his mum. I have been on this journey for a while, and I am so grateful. My life does matter and so does yours. This journey started close to thirty- years ago. I have taken my power back! I have released so much and I'm still releasing. In addition to the above steps, I spend a lot of time in nature. I still go to therapy as needed. I have mentors and coaches for the different parts of my life. I basically have a self-care team.

The woman I am today, loves herself, is at peace, full of joy and happiness. I choose to be happy and joyful. I choose to be silly and laugh a lot. I choose to dance like nobody's watching. I choose to be at peace. I choose to be me; I choose me each and every time. You get to choose you and how you want to be. Every day, I wake up, I take a breath and go into gratitude that I am still here. I am grateful that I have the power to choose me no matter what. You have the same power! Today, choose you!

REFLECTIONS

REFLECTIONS

Melba del Carmen Victoria Stetz

LTC (Ret.), Ph.D., BCN, BCB

"Melbita" was born on the beautiful island of Puerto Rico. A very smart and "hyper" individual, she was diagnosed with Attention Deficit Hyperactivity Disorder (ADHD) a relatively new diagnosis back then. A 'drop out' of pre-medical school and U.S. ARMY Veteran, she obtained three Psychology degrees, got licensed and become an officer.

LTC Stetz is a licensed work psychologist, a psychology professor, a certified life/work coach, a reiki master, and a board-certified neurofeedback and biofeedback therapist.

She is furthering her skills and gifts in psychic, mediumship, and healing work. Professor Stetz has published numerous peer-reviewed articles and chapters on her stress and coping studies. She just recently became a book best-author for *Winner's Mindset: Peak Performance Strategies for Success*.

You can find Dr Melba balancing her life between family, coaching, teaching, mentoring, writing, and speaking (Spanish/English).

https://drmelbastetz.com/

Killing Me Softly to Beam me up, Scotty!

BY MELBA STETZ, LTC (RET.), PH.D., BCN, BCB

"If you MUST plan to kill yourself... it is probably NOT your time."
— MELBA STETZ

My suicide story is, gladly, not a successful one. That said, I had perhaps thought my whole life about being dead. Yes, for over half of a century, I have often wondered about the purpose of my existence. However, I believe that my failure in killing myself has been due to a lack of a plan or someone stopping me.

I know that there are millions of people with way worse life experiences than me. However, I only know someone's whole story: mine. Therefore, I will only share here the parts of my life when I remember wanting to vanish. *Cautionary note*: I can't claim to be a "Star Trek" follower per se. When I was growing up in Puerto Rico (PR), everything was about "Star Wars." That said, when I did see Star Trek, I fell in love with the concept of being able to just: vanish and teleport to a better place. "Scotty, beam me up (or the other way around) was fabulous! Despite how cowardly and childish it might sound: I wanted to disintegrate into nothingness.

Most of the time, I wanted to kill myself because people didn't like me. The most influential people in my life didn't want me around. I intended to quit, stop, or just numb my emotions. I hoped to go where those who were hurting me couldn't find me. I imagined this 'somewhere else' as a magnificent place. Sometimes it was in the clouds. Some days it was in the stars. I could even go "there" when swimming or submerging underwater. In my dreams, I would just breathe and fly away to a place where I could be myself. No questions asked.

How can we prevent suicide? Why can't one suicide attempt be enough to this world to stop it? I mean, when I was a U.S. ARMY Research Psychologist, I would conduct studies on war fighters' stress. So many times, when discussing these results, there would always be individuals stating things like: "Well, there was only a 10% suicide rate." I would think (and carefully, say) "Only?" One person is enough.

There must be a difference between *living* and merely *existing*. So why do we give up on ourselves? Why do we attempt to numb our emotional pain with unhealthy (pro-dying) acts such as overworking, overeating, and under sleeping? Why do we learn to hate ourselves as much as others hurt us?

In the following pages, I will be describing some of my life and death experiences. First, I will change some names out of respect to privacy. Then, I will share with you some of my self-hating/ unhealthy habits. I call these: Killing me Softly behaviours). Yes, like the song's title "Killing me softly" song. Finally, I will talk about ways that have helped my mind, body, and soul (instead of asking Scotty to Beam me up!). Those are the ones that I suggest to my clients and students. Thanks for reading my story. I hope you can share yours with me one day.

AT HOME

My mother was a beautiful and loving lady. She came from a modest home in the U.S. Island of PR. She had hard-working parents and a roof to share with seven other siblings. "Mami" (Mum) had to work very hard to get a federal job as a Dietitian in "Nueva York" (NY). I mean, no doubt she was intelligent. However, English is still our second language. My father had a similar background but fewer siblings in Lima, Perú. He had a great heart as well. They met in a Veteran's Hospital in Manhattan (NY). She was a dietitian, and he was a medical resident.

After a couple of years, they got married and had my sisters. Unfortunately, they had gender socially imposed Hispanic and Catholic pressures at the time. Therefore, they ("had to") try again for a boy. My mum was familiarised with that concept as she was one of 7 sisters until her brother was born. I think it is also a survival mechanism to keep the father's/family (last) name: alive. Sadly, I came out as a girl. After trying one more time, my parents finally had "the boy."

I felt that once he was born, Mami dropped me like a hot potato. I had seen pictures of my parents taking care of me when I was little. However, my earliest memory was going to the store and having her ask me to choose one item. Minutes later, my brother pointed to a Michael Jackson poster. Wow! She ended up buying him the whole collection! Talk about posters, shirts, even a belt! It was evident to me that something was not right. I could see how frustrated she was with me and how her eyes would light up when talking to him.

ADHD?

Attention Deficit Hyperactivity Disorder (ADHD) was not a well-recognized disability diagnosis when I was growing up. Nevertheless, I kept hearing complaints about me having "too much energy" and not being able to "stay still." The sad thing is that most of what I recall are my mother's angry words.

Knowing that the person who brought you here didn't want you anymore was disheartening. These are the translations of some things that she would say to me: "You are so mean!" "You did that on purpose!" "You are so weird!" "No one can understand you!" "Get out of my face!" "Leave me alone!"

We Puerto Ricans are a culture composed of Taínos, Spaniards, and Africans. We have our spiritual practices as Catholicism and our "Vudú" (witchcraft). Perhaps that inspired her to constantly tell me the following words (surely, not a love spell): "Hija fuístes, madre serás. Como tu hiciste, peor te harán!' "Daughter you were, mother you will be. You will be worse than you did." I felt that there was no real emotional connection. My memories are mainly of talking to her while doing something else (typically for my dad or brother).

I was one of those kids that would question everything. I would say: "Papi (dad), why must we do that?" She would interject with, "Cause we say so." I would ask: "Mami, what did you cook? To which she would reply, "Food, and if you don't like it, don't eat!" Gladly, one of my sisters, "Doña (Mrs.) Mary" (our nanny), and my dad (when around) would be nicer to me.

SOME DEATHS

One of the earliest deaths I recall was when I was around nine years old. My father's dad, *Abuelo,* came to live with us after my grandma *passed away in Perú.* We would go to the beach and fill up buckets with sand. We would make sandcastles. However, you could hear him at night asking Abuela to take him with her. Apparently, she did. One day, my Judo class went to *El Yunque,* which is our rainforest. We were practising our *Katas* (forms)" sequence over floating rocks. Suddenly, I heard our Sensei (teacher) loudly calling one of my best friends: "Peter!" "Peter!" I was the smallest in the group, so the Sensei sat me on top of a big rock. We all kept calling Peter. Minutes later, what seemed like an eternity, they pulled him out of the water. He looked lifeless and purple. His uniform had gotten stuck on a branch. I felt so useless watching everything. It was a horrible day.

During a family vacation in Florida, my brother and I went to the hotel pool. Suddenly, some of the kids in the water started to scream out loud. I was one of those kids. All the parents came to that small pool to help us get out. Once out, we realised that one of the kids had drowned right after eating. I still remember feeling her lifeless hand in the water.

IN SCHOOL

When I was in high school, I liked this guy. I thought he liked me too, but I realised that he was just playing games. Therefore, my self-esteem was like a roller coaster. He would look at me, smile, and then push me away. However, at that time, it hurt a lot. When I finally moved on, I looked at the next potential source of love for my broken heart. He was more knowledgeable in the love department than I was. However, it was not a healthy relationship either. So, one day, I started cutting myself on the wrist. I was not successful nor told anyone at home. I am glad I did not have something sharper. That said, I still have the scars.

IN THE ARMY

When I first joined the military, I had just turned 19 and was very impressionable. During the training, I met this fellow student who looked like one of the superheroes I had seen on TV back in PR. By the end of many months of training, we both did not want to be apart. Therefore, we had this "great" Hallmark-channel type of idea of getting married! A year later, he was kicked out of the ARMY. We filed for bankruptcy, and I ended up miscarrying. How horrible is to have everything ready to welcome a baby for then bleeding it out of my system! We annulled our relationship. Well, I did after he even sold Puffy, the dog that I had brought from my island.

A few years later, a friend told me that a guy liked me. I was not that into him but, for some reason, felt "sorry" for him. We started hanging out. He was initially 'nice' and everyone "respected [feared] him." I thought it was because he was a very tall guy built like a football player. Remember Julia Roberts in "Sleeping with the Enemy?" Well, one day, he got mad at me and threw me against the wall. Gladly, I had finished that military contract. I ran to a neighbour's house, and Papi paid for the rest of my ticket back home.

Twenty years later, I met the love of my life. For close to three months, we had a living person in my body. We heard his/ her heartbeat in the hospital. However, one day during an ultrasound, I was told: "Sorry, but you're no longer pregnant. There is no heartbeat". I thought the machine was broken and asked for another one. No sound, nada. Years later, after painful fertility procedures, we decided to adopt. The baby was abandoned in a box when she was one day old. We were glad that no one hurt or killed her that day.

MORE DEATHS

While in my Psychology Master's classes, a few of us would meet to study right after our Practicum. Juan did not meet with us one day. His mother later told us that he kept saying that the beach was *calling him*. She thought that he just wanted to swim. He never came back. We believe that he was bullied due to his homosexuality. At that time, same-gender couples in a Catholic Hispanic Island were not well-accepted. Similarly, one of my professors died of acquired immunodeficiency syndrome (AIDS). It was so sad seeing him getting thinner and thinner every week. Then, one day, he did not show up to teach. Rest in peace.

As an enlisted soldier, I often had to give the US flag to the family of fallen soldiers. I would have to say something like this: *"On behalf of the President of the United States, the Department of the ARMY, and our grateful nation; Our country's flag is presented to you as a token of appreciation for (deceased family member)."* Everything would go by the book until I would say the name of their deceased loved one. We were not allowed to cry while in uniform nor with them. Our mission was just to follow the script and present them with our flag. Containing my feelings back was always a challenging task.

While doing a psychology study with a military surgical unit, I ended up visiting the morgue. Body parts looked like unassembled store mannequins. Later, I saw them also in Afghanistan (Operation Enduring Freedom). One night, they brought a couple of Marines who were blown up by an IED (improvised explosive device). Their rear ends looked like charcoal. I can still smell their burning skin.

In Afghanistan, we would also stop to salute cars transporting falling comrades on their way to the airport. In Iraq (Operation Iraqi Freedom), I saw a few raped / bullied / hazed soldiers ending up blowing up their brains in the field latrines. It was truly horrible.

I had a Sergeant working in my office on a virtual reality gaming project. One day, he asked me if he could leave early. A few days went by, and I learned that he was diagnosed with PTSD. He went to some classes but apparently would drink himself to sleep. One night, he went clubbing, drank a lot, and got into a fight. His body was found in the streets of Chinatown. When I gave the eulogy and saw his 4-year-old girl next to his ashes, I lost it. I started crying, and everyone else followed—sad day.

Probably my worst death experience (other than losing my mum to cancer and my father due to Hurricane María) was the one with my daughter. One night, our toddler was crying for my attention. I was on my computer and had seen her crying for a few minutes. I was going to stop and put her to sleep as I knew she was tired. However, she got quiet, I turned around, and she was turning purple. We called 911 and followed their guidance. We had an excellent Fire House Department nearby. They took care of our angel with an oxygen mask and drove us to the nearest military hospital.

PTSD?

One day, one of my doctoral students came to ask me why I often look "upset." He did not know of my chronic physical pain or work stressors. That made me upset. I thought he was "disrespectful" as he was an intern with a lower military rank than me. Therefore, I reported him to his direct supervisor. That said, since he was an outstanding officer and clinician, his comment stayed in my mind. I considered it as PTSD can be differentiated from Anxiety and Depression due to the anger/frustration component. However, I could not dare get seen then as Psychologists/ Mental health personnel are not expected to have mental health issues. Furthermore, I was not ready to lose my job having a toddler at home.

Another day after work, I drove to see my daughter's ballet practice. It was steps from a basketball court where a few teenagers were playing. There was a lady with a new-born in a stroller. We are trained to look for "worst-case scenarios." That means that we must be on the alert. I worried that the ball would hit either my 4-year-old or the baby. Therefore, I firmly yet politely asked the teenagers to be careful. Unfortunately, they ended up hitting the baby with the ball. I got upset and got right up in the face of the "punk-with-the-ball". I was in uniform wearing my deployment, Airborne, and Major identifiers. He said something brave to me (which I can't recall). I do remember me telling him: "Go ahead and hit me. I will then make sure that the MPs (Military Police) get up all over you!" The MPs came. Sat them down on the floor and took my statement. Afterwards, once at home and more relaxed, I realised that he could have broken my face.

Similarly, another day, there was a car driving very fast in the parking lot. We were with another couple walking nearby. He was so close to me that I went ahead and hit it with my hand (as if looking for a fight). Afterwards, again, I realised that I was not as strong as the car. I was getting like a superhero complex where I could end up dead.

I also started to get angry and frustrated with my family. I remember my sweet dear husband telling me one day: "Why do you treat me this way?" It was like we were living altered realities. That is the catch-22 of having ADHD and PTSD: you are stuck and numb. However, I was not diagnosed yet. There was (still is) a significant stigma about psychologists getting mental help.

One day, my husband was working in his office. He heard my daughter and me arguing about something. She and I talk in Spanish, so he does not always know what is going on. In the spirit of being a great father/protector, he ended up saying things that hurt me. Since it was not the first time, he talked to me like that, I got triggered again. I started thinking about how their life would be much better without me. Like that expression of "If you love someone, you must set them free". I thought again of how lucky Star Trek was with the "Beam me up Scotty" possibility. I just wanted to disappear. Somehow, I ended up curling up like a foetus in our closet until my hubby found me.

KILLING CANCER?

Upon retirement, I thought all my stress was under control. I mean, we had chosen to retire in beautiful Hawaii! A few years later, my teenager wanted to buy some clothes. I took that opportunity to make it another of what I call *mummy-daughter bonding time*. She wanted to go to "Pink", which is close to "Victoria Secret." We decided to try things on, like in our fashion show. All of a sudden, I felt like something hurt me while trying an intimate top. I thought it was a metal wire and told her that I would not get it. We ended up buying a few, eating ice cream, and everything was great.

Upon waking up, I felt something around my left rib. It felt like a marble ball. I asked my daughter, and she said that it felt like a ball. I remembered my cancer survivor sister's advice to go to the nearest military hospital immediately. I got in the car and called my husband on the way there. We all decided that if it was cancer, I would have surgeries, followed by chemo and radiation therapies.

I did not try to kill myself. I didn't have to. The mutant cells were going to do it for me. One night after chemo, I was so weak. It was Christmas, and I couldn't even open the gifts with my daughter. I could not even move. I thought: what if?

"KILLING ME SOFTLY" BEHAVIOURS

I believe that we can try to kill ourselves softly and slowly. That is what I have been doing. I was trying to escape from my pain with the following actions.

Over-Eating: When I would feel like my mum did not care about me, I would eat my feelings away. Yes, I would eat as much as my stomach could take the pain. I had to punish myself with physical pain when perceived as *not worthy*. I was trying to fill that emotional void by going to her small fridge *stash* of cookies. Filling up my stomach was taking the place of filling up my heart with her love. Her stash would make me feel closer to her, like back in her womb. It would also make me feel like I was sharing those cookies with her. On the other hand, I would feel like I was taking something from her, just like what I believe she took from me when reminding me of my ADHD *mishaps*. After my long and painful binges, I would just wear an oversized t-shirt hoping to cover it up. One day, I was even asked by a friend's mum if I was pregnant.

Over-Exercising: To counteract my overeating, many times, I would exercise, exercise, exercise! Mention a certification, and I probably have it: Zumba, Cardio-kickboxing, Yoga Sculpt, etc. Maybe I was hoping not only to lose the weight but also to collapse or break a bone. Or perhaps I just wanted to *go unde*r with surgical anaesthesia. However, my soul was not right, I was feeling hurt and empty.

Laxatives: My mum would keep diuretics and laxatives in her bathroom. I would take one of those when I could not get rid of the caloric "evidence" via purging or exercising. Another thing that somehow would make me more "like her."

Workaholism: My father was a workaholic. He would work twelve hours, six days a week. Interestingly, overworking involves being overtasked and being a poor time manager. In the Army, everything was *Hurry up and wait!* We had to be ready all the time or what we call *24-7*. Feel free to read my chapter *"Looking Back: From the Lab to Iraq. . . and to the Clinic"* on more of my early military experiences. That was part of my ADHD hyper-focus. I can't even remember how many times I travelled or deployed were sleeping was just a *luxury*.

Self-Medicating: Seeing so much death (e.g., burned kids in Afghanistan due to parents making bombs in their kitchens). Military daily exercise, combat boots, quick lunches, long meetings, and days can all translate into pain. That's why numbing our body with pharmaceuticals was a common thing. While in Basic Training as an enlisted and later on in Airborne (jump) School as an officer, my diet included black coffee and painkillers. No wonder why now I have ulcers. Same thing when having to wear that heavy "battle rattle" protective gear while deployed to Iraq and Afghanistan. The addictive "Vicodin" painkiller would do the trick when I could not take the pain anymore. Sometimes, having a drink or two would also help numb my mental and physical pain. Yes, many times too, I wondered what would happen if I mixed some of these drugs. But, many times, I just did not care.

THRIVING TOOLS

Below is what has helped me get over some of the experiences mentioned above.

Empathy and Forgiveness: I am a mother now. I know now how hard it is. I know my mum had a great heart and the best intentions. She was struggling with some anxiety and depression. I recently read some of her poems. Wow, how she suffered when losing her parents and many sisters. She also wanted to die! I was probably not that easy to raise either. Gladly, we got to sort it all out way before her passing. I now remember her by listening to her favourite song from Celia Cruz-: La Vida is a Carnaval (Life is a Carnival).

Grieve: Talk, listen to music, watch movies
- ✓ Music- I tend to listen to the following ones to help me re-connect:
  - Puff Daddy- I'll be missing you
  - Georgia Mass- Turn it over to Jesus-
  - Marc Anthony- Vivir mi Vida (Live my life)
  - Whitney Houston- I will always love you
  - Righteous Brothers- Unchained Melody
- ✓ Photos- Keep photos of your passed loved ones. Put a flower nearby. Maybe candles, rosaries, chakra stones, anything that makes it a nice place to be remembered.

Let go or let God: Sometimes, all we can do is breathe, ask God/ Universe, and hope/ pray for the best.

Self-Care, Self-Compassion: Remember that we were born alone (even twins) and will die alone. We are the most important people in this world. Just like putting the oxygen mask on a plane, if we don't care for ourselves, we can't take care of anyone else. We can't give what we don't have.

Think of your obituary: Write how you would want to be remembered. I know this sounds weird and hard to do! However, this exercise helps us put everything in perspective. Realise what matters in life as we will not take anything material with us. I think about how I would want my daughter to remember me. How will that help her the rest of her own life?

Be grateful and laugh often: It is very healing remembering the great things we have in life. These things do not have to be material. The following is a song that reminds me of my dad: Luther Vandross- Dance with my father.

Mindfulness, Meditation: Meditations and out of body experiences (e.g., dreaming) are great ways to temporarily deal with reality by "escaping" going back to the source of our existence. When we meditate or *Sit-in-the-Silence*, we are more aware of what is happening within ourselves: our mind, body, and soul. We look within. Time stops. We just listen to our breath and re-train our brain to hold off on thinking. The goal is to listen to our inner voice. We are wise in more than one way. Let's hear it.

Spiritualism/ re-think Death: Einstein once said: *"Energy cannot be created or destroyed. It can only be changed from one form to another."* I now believe in life after death. That is, I have been able to talk to my mum and others in my family who have passed. My mum was one of the first ones to come through! That is priceless. I am writing my own book on my experience. Feel free to ask me later about it.

Stay positive: We must keep ourselves happy. Be grateful. Count your blessings. That will keep up afloat any negativity. Law of Attraction suggests that we attract what we think. Therefore, start your day by raising your vibration. For that to happen, all you have to do is think of reasons to be grateful (e.g., being alive, having a car, etc.). Repeat if possible mid-day and before going to sleep. Like Suzanne Giesemann (Spiritual Medium) said: *"The Soul is awake- is the human who is asleep."* We can go from being Asleep (powerless victims) with a dualistic mentality of black and white; good/bad; heaven/hell to being Awake and Aware (and empowered), seeing everything/ everyone as one same unified energy. My former boss, Doctor Folen, used to remind us to be human *beings* and not human *doing*. Like Dr Zimbardo's Time Perspective Theory proposes: the past is gone, and the future is not here yet.

- ✓ *Sitting-in-the-Power* is another meditation technique where we expand our love and our soul to the whole world. It is very healing. All that we must do is sit comfortably, breathe deeply, expand our inner light/soul, and *let go*. Those who believe in something higher, *Let God/Spirit/Universe/etc*. Increase your vibration by being good and doing good now.

Biofeedback and Neurofeedback: I am board-certified in both Biofeedback and Neurofeedback. These modalities are about testing and training our brains by placing electrodes or sensors in different parts of our bodies to pick up nervous system readings. For example, we tend to live, in brain-waves language, in awake Beta (or High-Beta if we are stressed-out, anxious) waves. However, to feel more relaxed, peaceful, and inspired, we must start slowing down these waves' hertz Alpha and Theta (pre- and post-sleep state). If you don't have access to sensors, you can just place your index fingers to feel your heart (e.g., wrist, neck).

Journaling: Keep notes of your life journey. The process of writing is therapeutic. It does not have to be a Diary per se. You can also record it on your phone.

Walking, Yoga, Exercise: We all know the importance of moving to improve our circulation. Proper circulation helps cells get all the oxygen and nutrients needed to stay healthy. Circulation helps us also detoxify our bodies from impurities. It does not matter much which exercise you choose to do. I used to teach Zumba, cardio-kickboxing, and yoga. However, walking around my neighbourhood with my husband is priceless.

Talk, Psychotherapy, Coaching: It is essential to be humble enough to ask for help. Of course, we can always talk to our friends and our families. However, some topics could benefit from a professional and objective point of view.

Psychopharmacotherapy: Like food and exercise, some chemicals can improve our mood neurotransmitters (e.g., serotonin). Sometimes, we might need more help (e.g., while grieving). Do not be embarrassed by exploring different options.

Family and Friends Support: My parents were great people who taught me to stay optimistic.. One day as a teenager, Papi saw me crying for a boy. He nicely but firmly told me not to cry for them as they would come and go. On the other hand, he said that degrees, diplomas, certificates, achievements, and trophies would always be there for me. He taught me that we all fall but that we should not dwell on it. We must get up and move on! Maybe that is why I loved the ARMY slogan of *Be All You Can Be!* and Nike's *Just do it!* Similarly, my mum, before passing, told me that she admired me for speaking up. My brilliant husband has also helped by creating a family habit of going to bed early.

Share, Mentor, Teach, Coach, Write: I have published over 25 research peer-reviewed articles/ chapters on stress management with tools like Virtual Reality and bio/neurofeedback. However, as part of my continuous growth, I am now engaging more in journaling, blogging, and writing non-military chapters (like this one). I am planning to publish my own book before the end of this year - and you can do it too!

CONCLUSION

Suicide is no longer an option for me. Life can be beautiful if we let it be. No need for me to be beamed out of this world. I will enjoy my time here and go whenever I am supposed to. We can all do this! Feel free to reach out to me. Thanks again for reading.

REFLECTIONS

REFLECTIONS

REFLECTIONS

Vanessa Johnson

Vanessa "Fireball" Johnson, a native of New York with a flare of Southern-ness from South Carolina is the CEO of Vanessa Johnson Enterprises LLC which hosts other organizations such as The Fight Is Fixed™ LLC, Dunamis Dominion LLC, Sonship Publishing House, Camouflage Housing services and Dunamis Homes of Divine Intervention, Inc.

She is an ordained Pastor, Prophetess, and Life of Victory Strategist who uses practical principles from the Word to help people confront and overcome the traumas and obstacles they may be facing and bring them into a path of Victory.

She believes in taking these principles to the "streets"!

No One Heard My Cry Except Suicide

BY VANESSA JOHNSON
USA

Transitioning isn't easy when it's caused by the death of a loved one. Winter of 1986 didn't start out great as my grandmother became sick and passed away. Although at the age of eleven, I had decided to start a new chapter in my life in South Carolina, it was now ending abruptly five years later. Without a goodbye, I was about to leave a great school, great friends, great teachers and most importantly, a family that I considered not only to be my cousins but my sisters and brothers as well.

No one said the transition would be easy, but no one said it would take my life on an adventure as well. I'm enrolled in a new school, having to make new friends and get acquainted with new teachers. I am now no longer taking a big yellow bus to school; I'm standing in a strange train station waiting for a train to take me. The train platform is full of other teenagers, children and adults waiting for the train to get to their destination.

As I am minding my own business, waiting for the train, this handsome chocolate guy with a nice faded flat-top haircut comes walking over to me and says, "What's up, how are you doing?" I say, "Hey and I am doing fine". He introduced himself to me as well. As I thought this would be the end of the conversation, he continued to talk with me. It seems as if he was a natural born comedian because he kept me laughing. Oh yes! He was running a great game on me. The train finally came, and he talked with me until it was time for us to get off. He was a student at the same school. I was a newbie of course!

This school was much larger than the one I had just left in South Carolina. It was filled with many other ethnic groups, and I just couldn't seem to think how in the world I would fit in. I already had friends from around the neighbourhood I knew who went to the school. The others went to a different school so therefore it wasn't that hard to settle in. I am so thankful for the wonderful friends I made on 169th Street and Riverside Drive as well as Washington Heights.

Settling in the school was quick. I was introduced to other people and my association with others grew. I was placed in a co-op class therefore I was in school one week and on a work assignment the next week. I really enjoyed this. A different way of learning while gaining employable skills at the same time.

Each morning I would see this same handsome guy that kept me laughing and entertained on our way to school. A relationship began. Was I starting to fall in love? I believed so. I met his family, and he met mine and then the journey of this love relationship began or so I thought!

Why didn't anyone ever tell me about guys like him? Why didn't anyone teach me about things that should and shouldn't happen in a relationship? Why? Why? Why?

The relationship was great in the first few months. Then the relationship became controlling and verbally abusive. Why didn't anyone tell me about the warning signs of an abusive relationship? Why didn't anyone tell me about red flags? Why didn't anyone tell me? And then came the first slap! I held my face and cried! I was shocked and turned to walk away. He said, "I'm sorry, it won't happen again". I fell for it! Over and over again, the control, the verbal abuse, the physical abuse, and now fear.

I didn't know who to turn to. I didn't know how to tell anyone what was happening to me. I began to internalize everything that was happening to me. Who can I get help from? I was now in a position of shame and guilt and didn't know how to get out. I was stuck! Here I was at sixteen and a half years old and never experienced anything of this nature before and didn't have the courage to tell anyone what I was going through, so I stayed!

By the age of seventeen my life has been rough and distraught. I am now experiencing mental abuse on top of everything else. My self-esteem is at the lowest point and I'm crying out for help without anyone hearing or noticing my cry. I'm suicidal but I just don't know what to do! Contemplating but it's yet just still an idea in the back of my mind.

It was quite a few people that saw me going through who said, "Vanessa get out!" and "You are crazy for staying!". But what they didn't realise was that it was easier said than done. At this point I am now the main chick with him having many side chicks. Maybe this could be my way out! Nope! Now on top of all the control, physical, verbal and mental abuse, I must now have sex when I didn't want to. How much more was I to take? I couldn't even answer that question.

I didn't know what to do. I couldn't tell my mother, what would she think of me? I couldn't tell anyone because I was ashamed and fearful and now in a bondage relationship that I felt that I had to stay in. Who can I turn to without being judged? Who can I talk to? It was as if no one knew nor cared, but that was my own perception from the inside.

There were many more slaps, punches to the chest, verbal and mental abuses which were followed by him saying, "I'm sorry!" I kept overlooking what was happening as if it was my normal life and I just kept a smile on my face. Devastated because in my mind I'm wanting to be out of this relationship and free but then I find out that I am now pregnant. My life is now changing forever.

In my last year of high school, pregnant, abused, ashamed and embarrassed, I did my best to make it through. Somehow, I thought me being pregnant would stop the abuse. I don't know where that idea came from because it surely did not stop. I'm thankful for his family and my friends that really supported me through it all as much as they could.

Five and a half months pregnant and I can't take anymore. I'm tired and the idea of suicide has now become my one and only out. The pressure was unbearable. Each day I was thinking of ways to commit suicide. Silently crying without being heard. Although my unborn child brought joy in one way my reality of what was happening to me brought suicide in another.

Coming home from school one day and I had made the final decision as to how I was going to commit suicide. I did not tell anyone what I was going to do, I was just going to do it and be done with it all. No more pain for me and no pain for my unborn child.

I cried and cried and cried. The pain was talking louder than anything else to me. I was tired. I was unhappy. I was beat down literally and figuratively speaking. And I was angry! I wanted out of this life. I sat under my five-story window contemplating jumping out. I was ready to write a note to my mother explaining that life wasn't worth living anymore. That I was ready to go, and I was taking my son with me.

Whilst sitting under the window and getting ready to get up and open it, suicide spoke louder and louder and answered the call of my pain. I'm at a place where there will be no more pain. I was getting excited about it but as suicide spoke louder and I heard it, I also heard a still small voice saying, "Vanessa, you have someone on the inside of you to live for. Live this day and do not die!" The voice that changed my life forever.

I knew who it was but never heard Him speak to me. Although suicide spoke loud and clear, that still small voice was louder and much clearer than anything I had ever heard.

I broke down and cried. I began to rub my stomach and thank God for the unborn son that was living on the inside of me. A life that I would soon be holding in my arms and thanking God forever more because he saved my life and didn't even know it. Eventually, I got myself together and went about that day as if nothing ever happened. I graduated high school knowing that I had a new journey to embrace.

Months went by and my son was born. I was the happiest girl alive. Nobody knew what happened on that dark day in my life. I would look at my son and look up to heaven and say, "Thank you!" Tears of joy were running down my face. I was forever grateful for this new life, saving the one I felt was broken and unnecessary.

I stayed in the relationship for the next few years off and on while planning my get out, never to return. When I got to that place, I was with my second child. I was fighting back but internally I was in pain.

Finally, embarking on the seventh year of this relationship I knew I was finally ready to be free without ever having to look back. I went on to college and graduated with my Associates Degree. While in college I met my first husband, and it started a new chapter on my new journey.

As this chapter closes, I do want to say that many years later, that same handsome chocolate guy came back to me and apologized for all the abuse and wrongdoing he had put me through. Although I had forgiven him many years prior, the chapter had finally closed with an apology. I'm grateful to God for keeping me going through it all.

"And we know that in all things God works for the good of those who love him, who have been called according to his purpose." Romans 8:28 (NIV)

For that chapter in my life, this Scripture sums it all up. The fight was fixed, the outcome was already determined and I'm here to tell the story! God works everything out for the good of those who love Him; that includes failed relationships that the devil thought would destroy us.

While on my new journey, I began to heal myself from the inside out. It took months and years of work, but it was all worth it. The first thing I worked on was my attitude towards what happened to me and the individual who violated me. I fixated myself to believe that developing a new attitude on the perspective of what happened to me would change my outcomes in my life.

I asked myself, what level of boldness and confidence would I walk in knowing that I'm guaranteed to win? Knowing that I could not lose? What level of boldness and confidence would I walk in that no matter how powerful or how strong the enemy raises up in my life, no matter how many tricks he pulled, no matter what his advantage may seem to be, I would always be declared a winner?

To walk at this level of boldness and confidence I knew that victory is the attitude of faith! I learned that I had already won the fight before I ever stepped into the ring or on the battlefield.

"For whatever is born of God is victorious over the world; and this is the victory that conquers the world, even our faith." I John 5:4 (AMP)

The second part of my journey was to discipline myself and become determined to walk in my victory. It takes a disciplined person to manifest victory consistently in their lives. I believe we must discipline ourselves to believe the word of God regardless of our situations because our victory is from faith to faith, and that I must understand that faith is born of the word of God.

In 2 Kings 4, it speaks of a widow woman whose husband died and left the family in debt and the debt collectors were coming to take her children for payment. She sought out the Prophet to get guidance. She received instructions and the final instructions was for her to go inside her home, shut the door behind her, pour oil into her jars until the oil stopped flowing. I embraced myself with an awesome and dynamic story of victory, with discipline and determination. As the widow woman went in and shut the door, I had to do the same thing. I had to shut the door on doubt, fear, confusion, being led by my emotions. Sometimes friends and family members and life contradicted my faith and the word of God. This widow woman closed herself inside of her home and trusted the word of God spoken to her, with her faith leading the way.

This widow woman's victory demanded determination. She was determined that this would not be a one-time experience but a way of life. Even though that answer may be no, victory is that determination that stands at the door and continues to knock. Victory was my determination that heard criticism but kept on pressing.

Victory was my determination that said my life is not without problems but is a life that faces problems with the promises of the word of God. My victory is that faith clings to the promises of God until the problem is defeated.

To help me continue to walk in that level of boldness and confidence in that attitude of faith, I used the scripture below as my rear-guard.

2 Samuel 23:9-10 Next to him was Eleazar son of Dodai the Ahohite. As one of the three mighty warriors, he was with David when they taunted the Philistines gathered at Pas Dammim] for battle. Then the Israelites retreated, but Eleazar stood his ground and struck down the Philistines till his hand grew tired and froze to the sword. The LORD brought about a great victory that day. The troops returned to Eleazar, but only to strip the dead.

This story speaks volumes to me. Here is a man who became one with his sword. His hand grew tired and froze to his sword, meaning his hand became welded to his sword. He held on to the promise until the problem was defeated.

Eleazar stood his ground and struck down his enemies until his hand grew tired and froze to the sword. I find this a powerful revelation and believe that as we continue to stand with the whole Armor of God on, even though our weariness, if we stand our ground and let faith take over, we can achieve anything.

Allow your faith to manifest the victory that is already yours. Faith became my rear-guard because each day as I continued, and still continue, to be an overcomer I speak forth the word of God until I see what I have spoken over my life manifest. Knowing the power that resides on the inside of me and how to navigate it, is a gamechanger for my life.

The third part of my healing journey was to understand that the trial was working for my good. Victory is not never going through a trial but how you are going through that trial. Knowing that it's working for you should give you great joy.

In Peter 1:7 it states, "That the trial of your faith, being much more precious than of gold perisheth, though it be tried with fire, might be found unto praise and honour and glory at the appearing of Jesus Christ."

In 2 Corinthians 4:17-18 we are told "This light affliction which is but for a moment (worketh for us) a far more exceeding and eternal weight of glory, while we look not at the things which are seen but at the things which are not seen for the things which are seen are temporal but the things which are not seen are eternal."

The light affliction that I went through worked a far more exceeding and eternal weight of glory. That was good news for me to hear.

When I read Romans 8:28 – "And we know that all things work together for good to them that love the Lord and are called according to his purpose." I started to understand that my fight is fixed even though it may look bad, I knew that at a certain point the devil will go down because he has to!

For me this is the victory that over cometh the world, even when it comes to our faith. As long as we stay in the arena (battlefield or ring) of faith, I believe OUR victory is GUARANTEED!

The final part of my healing journey and continues to be is holding on to my faith. In this healing journey, I also understood that before the fight ever begins, God has already declared me delivered and victorious. My fight was never against my problems. It was against my faith! When the facts contradict what God has said, I had to fight to hold on to my faith in Him and what His word said.

Many of you reading this chapter and book are facing, have faced or possibly will face a situation in your life that seems to have come out of nowhere. I've learned that many times they are old problems that have resurfaced due to not being dealt with the first time, or not learning the lessons we needed to learn the first, second, third and many more times before.

The situation may feel unsurmountable, even avoidable and you may have tried desperately to find a way of escape and couldn't. The situations are there to help build our faith in God, and the enemy will use it to destroy our faith. We just have to understand that our fight is already fixed. The problem is only temporary. One important factor – it's not "what" has come against you but "Who" is actually with you. The battle is not ours; it is the Lord's, and we will not need to fight.

Find or deepen your faith, stand strong in it knowing that the fight is fixed. It's a battle that you have already won.

REFLECTIONS

REFLECTIONS

REFLECTIONS

ABOUT THE PUBLISHER

British boutique publishing services are offered by Author Coach, Dawn Bates, an extraordinary woman who specialises in changing the mainstream narratives through the art of literature. Titles published incorporate solo authors as well as a carefully chosen groups of individuals for a wide variety of anthologies in the realms of human rights, social change and cultural diversity.

As well as being an international bestselling author, writer, authority coach, educator and publisher, founder of *Dawn Publishing* Dawn Bates, specialises in developing brand expansion strategies and global visions, underpinned with powerful leadership and profound truths.

She writes for various magazines, and when not travelling or sailing around the world on yachts, she appears on multiple media channels highlighting and discussing essential subjects in today's society.

All the titles published under the *Dawn Publishing* brand bring together the multi-faceted aspects of the world we live in and take you on a rollercoaster ride of emotions while delivering mic dropping inspiration, motivation, and awakening. The books capture life around the world in all its rawness.

Discover more books from *Dawn Publishing* by visiting:
www.dawnbates.com/readers

www.ingramcontent.com/pod-product-compliance
Lightning Source LLC
Chambersburg PA
CBHW030258100526
44590CB00012B/437